THE DAWN OF
CIVILIZATION

THE DAWN OF
CIVILIZATION

4,000 – 500 BC

SEAN ELLERKER

Matador
9 Priory Business Park
Kibworth Beauchamp
Leicestershire LE8 0RX, UK
Tel: (+44) 116 279 2299
Fax: (+44) 116 279 2277
Email: books@troubador.co.uk
Web: www.troubador.co.uk/matador

ISBN 978-1783065-431

British Library Cataloguing in Publication Data.
A catalogue record for this book is available from the British Library.

Typeset in Aldine by Troubador Publishing Ltd
Printed and bound in the UK by TJ International, Padstow, Cornwall

Matador is an imprint of Troubador Publishing Ltd

For Edit, Emma and Lily

PROLOGUE

I magine a world devoid of virtually everything we take for granted; no countries or cities, no books, no money, no semblance of what we regard as civilization. This was the world of just six thousand years ago, inhabited by human beings with fundamentally the same mental and physical capacities as those who live today. Such an existence may seem incomprehensible now, but for the many generations of people who lived during the prehistoric era, life had always been this way.

For better or worse, the situation changed in the Fourth Millennium BC when the most advanced societies began to demonstrate astonishing levels of intellect and innovation, nurturing a propensity for progress that would change the face of the planet forever. As they entered the threshold of history, these great pioneers, our very own ancestors, embarked upon an incredible journey that still continues at a breathtaking pace.

The Ancient Near East, Egypt and Eastern Mediterranean

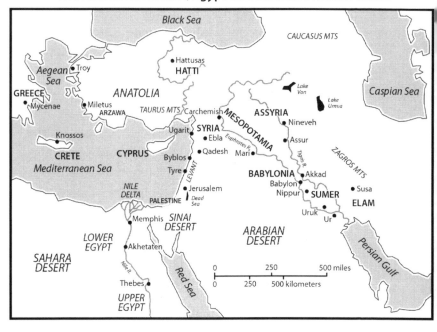

I

The dawn of civilization was made possible by the Neolithic Revolution; the gradual transition from hunting and gathering to agriculture that began after 10,000 BC. During this period, the domestication of animals and plants and the inventions of irrigation and the plough enabled the production of a steady food supply, with commodities such as cattle, sheep, cereals and vegetables available in abundance. As surpluses were accumulated, a global population of less than ten million people finally had the means to settle and grow. In each agricultural settlement, permanent dwellings were built in close proximity to each other, as the convenience and efficiency of farming meant that it was no longer necessary to forage across vast expanses of land for food and resources.

The process of managing food supplies was vital and societies adapted by allocating responsibility for controlling and distributing provisions to their most influential members. As these individuals assumed positions of authority, typically as chieftains or kings, the majority continued to work on the farms, while others specialised in crafts, assisting the farmers by making tools and storage pots. Social and economic organisation had begun and people became dependent upon each other, forming closely bound communities that shared customs, including language and religious practices. All over the world, these customs would evolve into strong cultural identities.

Of course, no society was fortunate enough to have access to every commodity that it needed. This encouraged trade with neighbouring communities and led to the emergence of professional merchants. As agriculture, metallurgy and craftsmanship became more sophisticated, the merchants were able to exchange a wide variety of goods and obtain both raw materials and luxury items from other regions. In the more productive settlements, where surpluses were plentiful, the ruling classes benefitted from the acquisition of precious metals such as silver and gold, enabling many kings, priests and nobles to become extremely wealthy. On the other hand, the temptation for envious tribes to exploit the wealth of their neighbours increasingly resulted in opportunist raids or full-scale war.

Despite this unfortunate side effect, the rapid development of these primitive societies is remarkable; an achievement that is rooted in the human aptitude for understanding the workings of the environment. It is no coincidence that the most productive settlements emerged in river valleys and coastal plains, where the soil was naturally fertile. This was perceptible in the earliest cradle of civilization, an area of rich agricultural land known as the Fertile Crescent, which included the Euphrates and Tigris rivers and the Levantine coast. As agriculture thrived, farming communities gradually appeared throughout the Near East; the wider region comprising Mesopotamia, the Levant and Anatolia. The earliest permanent settlements were mainly villages, although the Neolithic towns of Jericho and Catal Huyuk were home to thousands of people centuries before the first civilized societies.

There has been much debate over what constitutes civilization and many attempts have been made to classify the term, but in truth it has never been an exact science; more the imaginary line that is crossed when an established culture is capable of surviving and prospering within its own complex set of structures. Original civilizations evolved in diverse regions of the ancient world, virtually or entirely independent of each other; ranging from Mesopotamia, Egypt and Crete to the great river valleys of India and China and the coastlines of Mexico and Peru. The ideas emanating from these cultures would be relayed to other societies over thousands of years, recreated time and time again in different forms.

II

The world's first recognisable civilization appeared in the heart of the Near East, on the lush plains of Mesopotamia. Literally meaning 'between the rivers', Mesopotamia consists of the long stretch of land between the Tigris and Euphrates in what is predominantly modern day Iraq. Contrasting with the arid conditions there today, in the Fourth Millennium BC this land was exceptionally fertile and a variety of crops were grown, from wheat and barley to vegetables such as lettuce, onions and garlic. One of the prime locations for agriculture was the southern region of Sumer and it was the inhabitants of this area who took the lead in transforming their primitive settlements into civilized societies.

There is a great deal of mystery surrounding the origins of the Sumerian people. Some have suggested they were descendants of the native population, who were building temples in southern Mesopotamia two thousand years before the first cities. Others believe they were migrants from the north or east. It is certainly intriguing that their language bears no resemblance to those spoken in and around the Near East, where the main linguistic groups were the Semitic languages of Arabia (which had reached the Levant and northern Mesopotamia), the native language of Egypt and the Indo-European languages of southern Russia (which eventually spread into both Europe and Asia). In fact there are no significant similarities between Sumerian and any other known language, living or dead. In the absence of written records from this formative period, the mystery of their origins may never be solved.

Fortunately, the emergence of civilized society in Sumer has been preserved by archaeological and historical evidence. During the Fourth Millennium BC, at the beginning of the Bronze Age, the villages benefitted from rising food production and trade, enabling them to develop into flourishing city-states. The first and largest to emerge was Uruk, while others such as Ur and Larsa soon followed. These sites were located within a few miles of each other, but each maintained its independence and controlled the surrounding villages and farmland. To support their growing populations, the Sumerians invented the wheel and sail for speeding up the transportation of food and raw materials by land and river. Even as the increasingly arid climate reduced the extent of the natural flood plains, they adapted by digging canals to keep the land irrigated and maintain a water supply to the cities.

With the bustling city-states best placed to survive the drier conditions, there was an influx of people from the outlying rural areas and the city leaders soon realised that the process of rationing food and organising labour required more systematic methods. This culminated in the invention of writing. Originally made by inscribing simple pictures onto clay using reed stalks, the first written documents were lists of livestock and agriculture, compiled in Uruk in c.3300 BC. The script was called cuneiform and it gradually spread across the Near East, becoming prevalent in regions as diverse as Syria and Elam (now part of south-western Iran). Pottery and architectural styles were exported as well, together with bronze technology, as Sumer began to establish a cultural hegemony.

Initially this did not extend to political influence; the early Sumerian rulers were not kings in the normal sense, but religious leaders, best described as priest-kings, who ruled the land from their temples and claimed a divine-given responsibility to protect the people. As Sumerian society prospered, the wealth of the temples increased and the old designs were replaced with majestic buildings known as *ziggurats*, which consisted of step pyramids with shrines on top. Towering over the surrounding houses, they were generally positioned alongside the living quarters of the ruling classes and other important buildings such as the state granary. The temples formed the focal point of each community, with religion embedded as the most important aspect of public life.

In essence the Sumerians believed the Earth was a floating disc on water, ruled by the gods in the sky, with the spirits of the dead dwelling in the underworld below. Each city was built for a specific god and gifts were presented to him via his earthly residence: the temple. The gods were portrayed as human in appearance, but endowed with immortality and dazzling supernatural qualities. Originally at the top of the pantheon was Anu, god of the sky and patron of Uruk, although he was later upstaged by Enlil, god of the air and patron of Nippur. Also of importance was Enki, god of water, and Inanna, goddess of both love and war. All the divinities were feared, loved and, most importantly, never doubted.

In all probability, the deeply ingrained religious zeal of the Sumerian people was driven by the permanent state of vulnerability and fear that they found themselves in. The Mesopotamian rivers had fluctuating annual water levels, resulting in the permanent threat of both flooding and drought. Natural disasters caused by sandstorms were also frequent. Left in this powerless situation, the inhabitants of Sumer interpreted all acts of nature to be the will of the gods. Misfortunes such as poverty and disease were regarded as divine punishments for sins committed and the poor and sick were looked upon with condemnation and disdain. Needless to say, such uncompromising attitudes were commonplace in the ancient world.

By the Third Millennium BC, as the need to control farmland and trade routes intensified, competition between the city-states escalated into warfare. Out of necessity, the Sumerians elected warrior-kings who had a civil duty to protect their cities. Initially these kings continued to serve as priests in the temples as well, but as they were required to spend more time on the battlefield, the two institutions began to separate. Cities were fortified and royal palaces were erected by labourers and guarded by the king's armies. As the Sumerians became enamoured with the concept of kingship, they compiled a monumental *King List* which charted royal descent from gods to mortal kings. Many of the kings were fictional, with some of them said to rule for hundreds or thousands of years, but the latest entries were the first men to have their names preserved in history. The most famous inclusion was the legendary King Gilgamesh, who became the hero of the world's earliest preserved story, *The Epic of Gilgamesh*, written in c.2100 BC.

In theory, the leaders of the various city-states took it in turns to be crowned as the King of Sumer, but in practice there were regular disputes about who had the right to the title. Sumerian religion attested that the King of Sumer was chosen by the god Enlil, which meant that any king who took possession of Enlil's patron city, Nippur, had a strong claim to rule the entire land. However, counter claims were often made by the rulers of other prominent cities, such as Uruk, Ur and Lagash, and fierce competition developed between the city leaders. Of course, not all kings were tyrannical, power-hungry despots and many exchanged gifts and engaged in diplomatic relations, but the more ambitious among them sensed the opportunity to increase their prestige and personal wealth, and duly undertook military campaigns against their rivals.

As they marched across the countryside, the Sumerian armies came into conflict with foreign states, including the northern cities of Ebla, Mari and Assur, while their incursions also heralded the beginning of an epic rivalry between Mesopotamia and Elam. After a long sequence of local wars, the first ruler to subdue the whole of Sumer was King Lugalzagesi of Umma, a warlord who managed to overpower Nippur, Uruk, and all the other major cities by 2340 BC. Sadly for him, the first unified state in southern Mesopotamia lasted just twenty four years before he was defeated and humiliatingly left in a neck stock outside the gates of Nippur. His conqueror was Sargon of Akkad.

III

While the Sumerians were confined to the small pocket of civilization in southern Mesopotamia, many of the nomadic tribes who spoke the Semitic languages had begun a long process of migration from the Arabian Desert to the fertile regions of Palestine, Syria and northern Mesopotamia. These early Semitic migrants spoke Akkadian; a language related to Hebrew and Arabic that was destined to outgrow and outlive Sumerian. Yet for many years it was Sumerian culture that persisted in the Near East as the Akkadians willingly adopted their customs, religion and way of life. Indeed, this remained the case when control of the Sumerian cities passed to the Akkadian kings.

The background of Sargon, meaning 'the legitimate king', is hazy to the say the least, but it appears that he was of humble birth and rose up through the ranks in the Sumerian city of Kish, where many Akkadians had established themselves among the elite. Having been appointed Governor of Akkad (the city which gave its name to the Akkadian language) it appears that Sargon rebelled against his overlord in Kish and achieved independence in 2334 BC. After spending several years consolidating his rule and strengthening his army, he ultimately vanquished Kish and then marched onwards to Uruk, where he defeated the hapless Lugalzagesi in 2316 BC. Inheriting an integrated Sumerian state, Sargon proceeded to Ur, where he declared himself the King of Sumer. According to legend, he then travelled to the Gulf and washed his sword in the sea to symbolise his rule over the whole region, before journeying back up the Euphrates to his royal residence in Akkad.

The city of Akkad was located to the north of Sumer and gave Sargon an ideal strategic base for more ambitious conquests. The exact details of his subsequent campaigns are unclear, but it is known that he went beyond the northern cities of Mari and Ebla, as far as the Taurus Mountains in Anatolia, and that he ruled over every town and city within the basin of the Euphrates and Tigris rivers, seizing control of all river trade. In the east, he conquered Elam and made the small town of Susa its new capital. In the space of just a few years, Sargon had created the world's first empire.

Once the dust had settled, the king set his sights on consolidating Akkadian supremacy and displaced many local rulers with governors from Akkad. He even sought to unite Akkadian rule with Sumerian religion by appointing his daughter as the High Priestess at Ur, where she was ceremoniously married to the moon god, Sin. Notwithstanding his respect for Sumerian religion, Sargon's conquests ensured that Akkadian became widely spoken and was enforced as the official language in various parts of the empire. Akkad was the new seat of power in Mesopotamia and merchants brought riches to the city from miles around, including the distant land of Meluhha, which may have been a name for the Indus Valley civilization in India. Unrivalled in its wealth and prestige, Akkad eventually lent its name to the entire Semitic region of central Mesopotamia and future kings strove to achieve the unified title 'King of Sumer and Akkad'.

In a very short period of time, the political landscape of the Near East had changed dramatically, with many formerly independent cities now answerable to just one man: the mighty Sargon. Understandably there were feelings of resentment among the vassal territories and as the king grew old, revolts became increasingly common, leaving the Akkadian governors to work tirelessly to suppress them. Eventually the widespread resistance culminated in a mass revolt whereby several cities besieged Akkad with the intention of overthrowing the king, but even when faced with this concerted assault, Sargon fended off the enemy and died as the ruler of an empire. His name was preserved in Mesopotamian legend and his achievements set a benchmark for imperial rule that would endure long after his death.

Akkadian rule suffered a momentary setback when Sargon's successor was murdered in a conspiracy. In the absence of leadership at the head of the army, the empire was on the brink of collapse; however salvation arrived in the form of Sargon's grandson, Naram-Sin, a character of similar strength and ambition who came to the throne in 2254 BC. Meanwhile, Ebla had regained its independence, Elam had attempted to follow suit and aggressive tribes such as the Guti, in the eastern Zagros Mountains, were beginning to stir up trouble. Unrest in the vassal states had denied the Akkadians access to vital supplies of copper and tin from Anatolia, as well as desirable materials such as cedar wood from the Levant. Consequently Naram-Sin was immediately left with a choice to either relinquish the empire, or fight. As a descendant of Sargon, it will be of no surprise that he chose the latter.

With ruthless efficiency, the Akkadian king seized control of Elam and wreaked destruction in Mari and Ebla until they surrendered. He then led his army as far as Anatolia, ordering his subjects to erect statues of him as he marched through their lands. Naram-Sin's successes and unwavering arrogance quickly invoked resentment in the other major cities, and accordingly they mustered coalition armies, led by the self-proclaimed kings of Kish and Uruk. Every major city in Mesopotamia took part, all venting their anger against enforced Akkadian rule, and yet somehow, as they had done in the name of Sargon two generations earlier, the Akkadian forces were able to resist the onslaught and defend their king. Brimming with pride, Naram-Sin proclaimed himself the 'King of the Universe' and took the extraordinary step of claiming divine status; a truly shocking assertion in a society where kings were regarded as mere shepherds of the gods. Indeed, despite the remarkable successes achieved by Naram-Sin, the concept of divine rule never won the hearts and minds of the Mesopotamian people and many communities were dismayed by his outrageous and unholy claims.

Nevertheless, Naram-Sin's position was so secure that he remained in control of the empire for the rest of his days. The importance of his personality was emphasised by the speed of decline in Akkad after his death in 2218 BC; during the reign of his son, Sharkalisharri, Mesopotamia was overrun by hordes of Elamites, Guti and Syrian nomads. All sense of order was lost and the whole of Sumer and Akkad descended into anarchy. Eventually the Guti tribe asserted their authority, but their barbaric dynasty bore little resemblance to the empires that preceded it and many Sumerian and Akkadian cities regained their independence. The poor leadership and administration of the Guti led to a decline in both food production and trade, resulting in a brief dark age in Mesopotamia that lasted for nearly a century.

IV

The cities of Akkad had been worst affected by Gutian rule and it was the Sumerians who eventually rose up against their overlords in 2120 BC. Utu-hegal of Uruk led the resistance and restored Sumer's independence by capturing and executing the last of the Guti kings, but just eight years later he was supplanted by his own governor in Ur; an opportunist general by the name of Ur-Nammu. This was the beginning of the Third Dynasty of Ur, so named because it was officially the third time the ruler of this city had assumed the Sumerian kingship. Having had the title 'King of Sumer and Akkad' bestowed upon him by the city's priesthood, Ur-Nammu banished the Guti from Sumer, pursued them into the mountains and proceeded to raid the neighbouring state of Elam, where he captured the city of Susa.

To minimise the threat of rebellion, Ur-Nammu decreed that only the regions of Sumer and Akkad were to be directly governed, while relations with the rest of the Near East were to be maintained through diplomacy and marital ties. The exception to the rule was Elam, which was occupied by the army. Although the scale of the empire was smaller than those of Sargon and Naram-Sin, Ur-Nammu's more conciliatory attitude to foreign policy was complemented by some progressive domestic policies which provided much of the stability that previous regimes had lacked. Intensive building work was commissioned, including new canals which enabled more land to be irrigated and sturdier town walls that provided greater security for the urban populace, while additional income was generated by tribute collections, mainly in the form of cattle and sheep. The king himself was showered with gifts and took advantage of his new-found wealth by remodelling the royal palace.

A long period of peace and prosperity followed, during which arts and crafts flourished and rebellions were few and far between. To many Sumerians, it must have seemed that they were finally back in favour with the gods. That said, life was still a struggle for most people, even in peaceful times. Both traditional farmers and craftsmen, as well as the numerous female factory workers who produced goods ranging from textiles to flour, only received small rations from the state and were often left indebted to private merchants. To cover these mounting debts, men were compelled to rent out their wives and children as servants for the wealthy. Even at this early stage of civilization, class divisions were distinct and extremely hard to break away from.

Although times were hard for many ordinary citizens, the wealth of the state was maintained by its rulers, whose duty was to protect the people from disasters such as famine and invasion. In practice, they often achieved these objectives by going on the offensive. Ur-Nammu was killed in battle against the Guti in 2095 BC, but was succeeded by his equally capable son, Shulgi, who avenged his father's death by winning a series of encounters in Gutian territory. He also made inroads against the Hurrians in northern Mesopotamia, where Sumerian trade routes were threatened. The effectiveness of Shulgi's military campaigning was improved by the creation of a standing army at Ur and it was during his reign that the empire reached its peak, with virtually the whole of Mesopotamia forced to swear allegiance to the Third Dynasty of Ur. Buoyed by his achievements, Shulgi followed the example set by Naram-Sin and proclaimed himself a god, insisting on being worshipped throughout the land.

The kingship passed smoothly to Shulgi's eldest son, Amar-Sin, and later to his younger son, Shu-Sin, but problems were beginning to surface. Although the events are obscure, it appears that Ur was badly hit by famine; a disaster that encouraged the emerging city of Isin to declare its independence. To make matters worse, a new peril from the west threatened to shake the empire to its foundations. The Syrian nomads who had previously partaken in the destruction of the old Akkadian Empire were collectively known as the Amorites and by the time of Shu-Sin's accession in 2037 BC, they had grown tired of answering to the King of Ur. The Amorites travelled around the countryside seeking new pastures for their sheep and were by all accounts regarded as uncivilized barbarians by the Sumerian people.

Shu-Sin was acutely aware of the threat that they posed and built a large fortified wall to the north of Ur to discourage an invasion. This postponed the inevitable for a while, but during the reign of his son, Ibbi-Sin, the determined Amorite forces broke through the wall and began to cause mayhem throughout Sumer. Panic ensued in the villages and many people fled their farms to seek protection behind the nearest city walls. When the King of Ur was unable to come to their rescue, the other cities of Sumer and Akkad decided to fend for themselves. The whole country was now at the mercy of the Amorites; or any other state that had the courage to take advantage.

Indeed, watching these events from afar, the Elamites were not about to miss a golden opportunity for revenge and as soon as Ur's defences were breached, Elam declared its independence and prepared to attack. The Elamite state, stretching from the city of Anshan in the south-eastern Zagros Mountains to Susa, 150 miles east of the Tigris, was an age-old rival to its Mesopotamian neighbours, although until now it had generally been on the receiving end. Elam's origins and much of its history remain elusive, but its people practised a culture that was distinct from those of Mesopotamia, worshipping different gods and speaking a language unrelated to both Sumerian and the Semitic languages. Past events had cultivated much resentment against Sumer and the Elamites relished the opportunity to fight back. In 2004 BC Elamite forces stormed into Ur and inflicted a heavy defeat on their oppressors, taking Ibbi-Sin prisoner in the process. In a cruel act of vengeance, they burned the city to the ground and carried its distraught king back to Elam where he died alone in poverty and exile.

Overrun by the Amorites and crushed by the Elamite army, the Sumerians were overwhelmed and never recovered from this devastating sequence of events. A large number of Amorites began to settle in the region amongst the Akkadians and from thereon it was the Semitic-speaking peoples who held sway. The Third Dynasty of Ur had suffered the same fate that would await so many empires in the future; territorial expansion is one thing, but maintaining order in resentful conquered lands is another thing entirely. Yet the Sumerian legacy would persist; their culture and religious practices were readily adopted by the Amorites, just as they had been by the Akkadians, and would long outlive the political influence of their people.

As Mesopotamia entered the Second Millennium BC, Sumer and Akkad reverted into independent city-states. King Ishbi-Erra of Isin, the strongest city at the time, claimed direct succession from the kings of Ur, but was unable to acquire enough clout to enforce a new empire, despite bringing about the end of the Elamite occupation. Isin's pretentions were challenged by its main rival, Larsa, and for decades the two cities fought for supremacy and the favour of the priesthood at Nippur. At the same time, Amorite influence deepened and before long their chieftains seized control of Uruk and Kish. Yet it was to be another city that would finally give the Amorites the power they craved. In fact, this was no ordinary city, but one of the most magnificent and influential ever to exist, whose famous name would inspire both kings and nations for centuries to come.

V

The great city of Babylon was originally one of many small and insignificant Akkadian villages which had already been established by the reign of Sargon in the late Third Millennium BC. Babylon's destiny changed when the first Amorite dynasty was founded there in 1894 BC and it gradually developed into a major urban centre, easing its way towards recognition and respect from the established Mesopotamian cities. Babylon is translated from Akkadian as 'The Gate of the Gods' and under Amorite rule it would soon appear to live up to its name. Situated near Kish in central Mesopotamia, the location of the city was fortuitous as it was near to the principal Mesopotamian trade routes and the point where the Tigris and Euphrates were closest together, enabling relatively easy access to much of the Near East. This was particularly useful as the site lacked natural resources such as metals and timber.

The situation was clearly favourable for the city's leaders and while Isin and Larsa continued to get at each other's throats, Babylon began to absorb more and more of its adjacent territory. By the time the Babylonian army approached the sacred city of Nippur, the leaders of the other Sumerian cities were compelled to stand up and take notice and Larsa in particular engaged in a series of battles with its new rival. Larsa's cause was aided by the accession of Rim-Sin, a dynamic king of Elamite origin who had, bizarrely for an Elamite, adopted Sumerian culture as his own. In 1793 BC, Rim-Sin was able to conquer Isin, meaning that Babylon alone blocked Larsa's passage to dominance in the regions of Sumer and Akkad. Unfortunately for Rim-Sin, his plans were scuppered by an immensely gifted Babylonian king who was keen to pursue his own ambitions. His name was Hammurabi.

One of Hammurabi's many qualities was patience and for the first thirty years of his reign he allowed Rim-Sin to dominate the region, confident in his belief that Larsa was not strong enough to overpower Babylon. Further afield, there were other dangerous states, such as the Kingdom of Mari in the north. There was a brief period of upheaval in Mari when the King of Assur, Shamshi-Adad, seized the throne and granted it to one of his sons. However, following his death in 1775 BC, the kingdom was reclaimed by the rightful heir, Zimri-Lim, who returned from exile to inherit a wealthy realm that covered much of northern Mesopotamia. Further antagonists were located in the east; especially the city of Eshnunna, located just across the Tigris, and the ever-present threat of Elam further to the south. Surrounded by hostile lands, Hammurabi was in no position to commit to war on several fronts, so initially he focused on strengthening the kingdom's defences, in particular by increasing the height of the city walls.

In the meantime, identifying Mari as the most powerful of these rival states, Hammurabi entered into diplomatic relations with Zimri-Lim and they soon became closely acquainted, frequently exchanging gifts and letters. Importantly, Mari could now be trusted not to take advantage should the bulk of the Babylonian army be deployed in the south. Hammurabi may have been planning to launch a southern offensive at this point, but in 1764 BC Babylon came under an unexpected attack from a coalition army led by the leaders of Elam and Eshnunna. A hasty alliance was agreed with Larsa, but the wily Rim-Sin was reluctant to send his troops into battle and deliberately left the Babylonians to fend for themselves. The invaders were kept at bay by the city's defences, but their audacity had convinced Hammurabi that it was time to seize the initiative once and for all.

Military preparations were intensified and a year later the Babylonians launched a blistering attack on Larsa, decisively defeating the aging Rim-Sin who had failed to keep his word.

Enraged by the events of the previous year, Hammurabi proceeded to lead his troops along the Tigris where they routed the Elamite army and mercilessly crushed the city of Eshnunna. The rampaging king was in no mood to stop there and, taking his ally completely by surprise, he turned on Zimri-Lim and ordered his men to destroy the city of Mari and set fire to the royal palace. Taking no chances, not even with his own ally, Hammurabi had timed his onslaught to perfection, decimating his strongest rivals and ensuring that Babylon would be unchallenged by anyone close enough to pose a threat.

The Babylonian Empire encompassed most of Mesopotamia and the neighbouring states; only Elam and parts of Syria held any degree of independence and even they were only spared because they were sufficiently weak or far enough away not to pose any problems. For all intents and purposes, Babylon held the seat of kingship in central and southern Mesopotamia on a permanent basis and was to become the lifeblood of Mesopotamian civilization. Because of Babylon's role in restoring peace and prosperity to the region, the local people affectionately embraced the city and its heroic king. The ancient region of Sumer and Akkad was reunited and henceforth became known as Babylonia.

Despite his proud Amorite heritage, Hammurabi was keen to promote Sumerian religion, but in order to confirm his own city's ruling status he had to initiate a momentous change. In a shrewd theological move, he ordered his priests to declare that, for the good of the people, the god Enlil had allowed Marduk, the patron god of Babylon, to assume leadership of the pantheon. This ensured that Babylon would be regarded as both the political and religious capital of Babylonia. Religion continued to play a leading role in the lives of the Babylonian people, with festivals and rituals occurring throughout the year, but crucially Marduk was now worshipped as the pre-eminent deity. Conspicuously, Hammurabi never claimed to be divine and instead respected the ancient dogma that the king's purpose was to serve the interests of the gods. This set a precedent in Mesopotamia and future Babylonian kings tended to resist the temptation to seek divine status.

Having bolstered the unity and faith of his people, Hammurabi devoted the rest of his reign to creating a more just society. The most important of his initiatives were the infamous *Codes of Law*, which he etched onto a stone slab with the intention of preserving them after his death. They consisted of a long list of crimes and punishments; for instance, 'If a man has stolen goods from a temple or house, he shall be put to death' and 'If a man's wife, for the sake of another, has caused her husband to be killed, that woman shall be impaled'. Such punishments may seem excessively harsh to the modern reader, but the declaration of the laws was a significant step towards providing a more secure way of life for the masses. Hammurabi presented himself as a man of the people who could be trusted to look after their interests and ardently pursue the course of justice. In both war and peace, there is little doubt that Babylon owed its rise to the ingenuity and hypnotic personality of its famous king.

It is perhaps for this reason that, following his death in 1750 BC, the power of the city slowly began to diminish. Hammurabi's son and heir, Samsuiluna, struggled to contain revolutionary movements in the south and rebels in Nippur led the dissension from Babylonian rule. Replicating his father's unyielding fighting spirit, Samsuiluna ensured there would be no total collapse and the northern part of the empire stayed remarkably intact; however the loss of the rich Sumerian heartland was a bitter blow. A string of disastrous domestic policies did not help matters. To compensate for the loss of the southern territories, Samsuiluna's successors tried to increase agricultural production in the remaining fields, but this only served to diminish the fertility of the soil and led to a food crisis. With the farmers unable to make ends meet, private merchants were permitted to provide them with emergency loans that they could never realistically repay. Babylon had deteriorated from being a thriving and stable realm to a wretched land, ridden with starvation and debt.

At this stage, even the leadership of the Amorites began to look vulnerable. In southern Mesopotamia, an independent state known as Sealand consumed large tracts of territory and an attempt to overthrow the Amorite king seemed likely. However the final blow to Babylon came completely out of the blue from an altogether unexpected source. In 1595 BC, King Mursilis of the Hittites, an Indo-European dynasty from Anatolia, made an astonishing raid down the Euphrates and, with virtually no resistance, sacked the city of Babylon and plundered its treasures. Had the Hittites decided to stay and rule Babylonia for themselves, the entire history of the Near East could have changed forever, but Mursilis departed as swiftly as he had arrived and the vacant seat of power was instead left at the mercy of the Kassites, another ambitious tribe with Indo-European influences. With Amorite rule abolished and the city's defences in tatters, any lingering doubts had been dispelled: the golden era which began with the reign of Hammurabi had come to a decisive and ignominious end.

As humbling as this experience was, it was not the death knell of Babylon; the legacy inspired by its famous king had overseen the city's transition from obscurity to greatness and it remained the focal point of Mesopotamia for centuries to come. Subsequent generations of Babylonians made incredible advances in subjects such as astronomy and mathematics, not to mention the practice of law. People from miles around thanked the gods for giving them such an inspirational role model and in the not too distant future, under the guidance of a new dynasty, they would once again rise up in the name of their beloved Marduk. Yet for the time being the story of Mesopotamia must come to a close; by the time of the Hittite raid on Babylon, other civilizations had also emerged and developed in fascinating ways.

VI

A s the Mesopotamian societies blossomed between the Euphrates and Tigris, important developments were simultaneously taking place in the valley of the Nile. Neolithic settlements appeared in the region of Upper Egypt (the southern, higher part of the Nile's course) in c.5000 BC and spread into Lower Egypt soon afterwards, eventually leading to the foundation of towns and villages which co-existed with those in the Near East. It appears that at least some contact was made between the two regions as Mesopotamian influences were evident in Egyptian art and architecture; however political relations between them remained non-existent for many years and their cultures evolved in very different ways. With its buildings and artefacts still capturing the imagination of visitors today, the unique and alluring civilization of ancient Egypt makes for a wonderfully compelling story of its own making.

Egyptian prehistory reached its climax with the unification of Upper and Lower Egypt in c.3100 BC. Although the precise sequence of events is unclear, it seems that the cluster of towns and villages in each half of the country were ruled by two competing chieftains who fought between themselves for control of the land. Eventually it was the southern army that triumphed and the leaders of Upper Egypt became the first kings to preside over the whole country. The first capital was founded in the Nile delta at a fortified site known as the 'White Walls' which grew to become the city of Memphis. Although the royal tombs were usually located at Abydos in Upper Egypt, the choice of a site in Lower Egypt as the new capital demonstrated the eagerness of the southern leaders to appease the defeated northerners and seal the permanence of the union.

The identity of the first king of Egypt has been the subject of much debate and the names of Scorpion, Narmer and Menes have all been suggested. The general consensus is that King Scorpion reigned first but that the final unification was achieved by a ruler who was known as both Narmer and Menes. Indeed, it was King Menes who was identified as the founding king of the First Dynasty by Manetho, a classical historian. Manetho's thirty one dynasties were broadly grouped into the Early Dynastic, Old, Middle and New Kingdoms, separated by intermediate periods where the unity of Egypt had been broken. The unity of the country was far from assured in the Early Dynastic period and ruling a country of over a thousand kilometres in length was no easy task, but for the next five hundred years, Menes and his successors laid the foundations of Egyptian civilization for the Old Kingdom and beyond. Even the frequent wars with Libya to the west and Nubia to the south were born in this early stage of Egyptian history, as were the first tentative trade relations with communities in Syria and Palestine.

King Menes appears to have been succeeded by King Aha (although this may have been yet another name for Menes and Narmer) and then by King Djer, who built the first palace at Memphis. As the Egyptian kings began to take advantage of their power and wealth, one of Djer's successors, King Den, decided to pursue a more aggressive foreign policy, crossing the eastern Sinai Desert to the Levant and bringing back a harem of Asiatic women for his own pleasure. Another practice to emerge during this period was the embellishment of the king's tomb with luxury goods for his use in the afterlife. In fact it was not just goods that were left in the tomb; family members, servants, entertainers and pets were all sacrificed, probably by strangulation, and then buried alongside the king so that they could continue to serve and please him after death.

The main focus in the Early Dynastic period was the preservation of peace between the two regions of the country, in what remained a fragile balancing act. King Den created the post

'Chancellor of Lower Egypt' to prevent rival factions from appearing in the north, while he also created the double crown, combining the red and white colours of north and south. King Khasekhemwy continued the process of centralisation by implementing economic and political reforms to maximise the generation of income from taxation and foreign trade expeditions. Records were kept by scribes, who wrote in hieroglyphics; a pictorial form of writing that was inscribed onto a paper-like material called papyrus, made from a plant that grew in the Nile delta. As the administration of the country became progressively more efficient, Egypt grew in prosperity and its kings began to apportion their wealth to state enterprises, usually in the form of grandiose building projects. The kingdom was on the verge of becoming a cultural phenomenon, unrivalled in its extravagance by any other state in antiquity.

The motivation behind Egypt's great cultural achievements predominantly derived from religious and mythical beliefs, deep-rooted in the prehistoric past. Egyptian religion was extremely complex and it would take entire books to describe all the aspects of the celestial hierarchy, but it is important to provide at least some impression of the theological framework that guided people's lives. Essentially there were three cosmologies, all closely linked and containing many of the same myths and deities. The first appeared in the city of Heliopolis in Lower Egypt, now a suburb of Cairo. The universe was said to have been formed from a liquid element known as *Nun*, or *Chaos*, which continued to exist outside the universe and contained weak souls such as still-born babies or souls which had not been given proper funeral rites. In the distant past, the sun god, Ra, emerged from the liquid element upon a mound of sand and from his own seed produced four generations of gods that would shape the earth and its elements. The final generation comprised two female deities, Isis and Nephthys, and two males, Osiris and Seth.

Osiris was the first mythical king of Egypt but was killed by his jealous brother, the infertile Seth, who seized the throne for himself. However, Isis later gave birth to Horus, a posthumous son of Osiris, and the young pretender eventually persuaded the elder gods to grant him the kingship. Meanwhile, Osiris became the ruler of the Kingdom of the Dead, a role that continued to be important throughout Egyptian history. Ra retained his status as King of the Gods and every night made a dangerous journey through the underworld before returning the next day, supposedly visible on earth through the daily cycle of the sun. On one of these journeys, Ra lost an eye and had to replace it with a substitute, only for the missing eye to reappear and shed tears of pain when it saw its replacement. These tears fell down to earth and became the people of Egypt.

In the city of Hermopolis in Upper Egypt, a second cosmology emerged. In this version, four divine couples, in the form of frogs and serpents, created an egg from the liquid chaos. A mound of earth appeared from the liquid, upon which they placed the egg. When it hatched, the sun emerged. The four couples each represented an element: Nun and Nunet were the liquid chaos, Heh and Hehet were water, Kek and Keket were the darkness, and Amun and Amunet were invisible. In the Middle Kingdom, the hidden god, Amun, was elevated to the head of the pantheon by the priesthood in Thebes, the principal city of Upper Egypt, and was worshipped ardently by kings and nobles across the south of the country.

The third cosmology developed in Memphis during the Fifth Dynasty and combined aspects of both the Heliopolitan and Hermopolitan systems, while raising the status of Ptah, a local deity. Ptah was the patron god of craftsmen and was said to have created mankind on his potter's wheel. He was succeeded by Ra, the sun god, Shu, god of the air, Geb, god of the earth, and then Osiris, Seth and Horus, in keeping with the traditions of Heliopolis. Eventually the kingship was passed down to the 'companions of Horus' who presided over the transition from gods to men. King Menes was the first of these earthly rulers, receiving the blessing of Horus himself.

Egyptian religion was constantly in flux and the exact combination of beliefs was variable depending on the time and place. Nevertheless, the names and attributes of the gods were stable and deities such as Ra, Horus, Seth and Osiris were continually worshipped across the land. Given the widespread belief that the kings of Egypt were direct descendants of the gods, it is unsurprising that the notion of divine rule became entrenched in Egyptian culture. The kings were worshipped as incarnations of Horus and after death they became affiliated with Osiris in the Kingdom of the Dead. The manifestation of Horus was the falcon and images of the bird were frequently associated with the Egyptian kings in paintings and sculpture. At the same time, from the earliest years of the Old Kingdom, the king assumed the role of Ra's representative on earth as the sun god watched over him from the heavens.

Despite the pre-eminence of Horus and Ra, the entire pantheon was respected and, as in Mesopotamia, there were numerous local gods that represented villages, towns or cities throughout the country. It was the king's duty to pay homage to all these deities, so not to invoke their wrath. Egyptian religion was so layered and multifaceted that a huge proportion of time was devoted to rituals, prayers and honorary building work. The whole purpose of life was to serve the gods and the best way to achieve this was to show unwavering dedication to the divine king and to prepare him properly for the afterlife. The role of the king was to ensure the protection of the people and to carry out the will of the gods, first and foremost by building temples and filling them with riches. This was essentially the relationship that shaped the history of Egypt for three thousand years.

VII

The Old Kingdom began in the early Bronze Age with the Third Dynasty and reign of King Djoser in 2667 BC. The new sovereign inherited a united and economically sound country that had been organised methodically by his predecessors. He lived in a mud-brick palace, surrounded by his personal harem, although he followed tradition by selecting a principal queen to be his main consort with responsibility for providing his heirs. The accepted practice was for the king to have children with several wives and if his first wife was unable to provide an heir, a successor would be chosen from one of his other sons. Strangely, in the event of the queen's death, it would often be their daughter, the princess, who would take her place. Incestuous relations appear to have been common in the royal household.

On the other side of the palace were the king's advisors, of whom the most prominent were the two *viziers* (one for Upper Egypt and another for Lower Egypt) who controlled everything from the economy, irrigation and agriculture to upholding the law and building the royal tombs. The viziers were supported by local governors, the *nomarchs*, who controlled the provinces, or *nomes*. In theory the king only retained direct control over religion and the military, although in reality he had unlimited powers if he chose to use them. Also employed by the state were an assortment of craftsmen and artists who were regularly commissioned by the king, and numerous scribes who were required to study a range of subjects including writing, accounting, history and architecture.

At the bottom of the social hierarchy were the thousands of peasants who grew crops by the Nile and were called upon to erect the state buildings and enlist in the army when required. They formed the bulk of society and were forced to toil long and hard for the king and his nomarchs. Yet despite their hardships, there was little dissent among the people because the king was widely regarded as their divine protector who guaranteed the changing of the seasons and the water supply to the Nile. This also meant there was no need for policemen. If any desperate souls did break the law, their punishment was forced labour in the mines, exile to the distant fortress of Tjaru, or simply to have their noses cut off.

The king had control over an absolute state, exercising his will without any semblance of opposition. His powers were bestowed upon him at a coronation that officially took place in the heavens and unlike most of the Mesopotamian rulers, who were regarded as servants of the gods, the Egyptian kings were acknowledged by both the priesthood and public as gods in the form of men. As there was no tangible threat to Egypt's borders throughout most of the Old Kingdom, there was no reason for anyone to doubt the invincibility of the king and the Egyptian people maintained the conviction that their country was the centre of the universe.

Having inherited such a secure position, King Djoser was free to embark upon a spectacular building programme that would permanently alter the Egyptian landscape. This included the construction of the first step pyramid; a huge edifice made entirely of stone which contained the burial chamber that would become the king's resting place. The design was attributed to an architect by the name of Imhotep; an exceptionally talented individual who also served as the Chancellor of Lower Egypt and the High Priest of Heliopolis, and was said to have been both an astronomer and one of the first pioneers of Egyptian medicine. Imhotep was eventually deified and worshipped as a local god in Memphis.

Another prominent figure in the Old Kingdom was King Sneferu, who founded the Fourth Dynasty in 2613 BC. Respected in both life and death, many of his successors believed him to be the ideal monarch and strove to emulate his ways. Sneferu was a warrior king who undertook several expeditions beyond Egypt's borders, mainly to acquire the capital that would fund the construction of new pyramids and temples. Of course the other vital ingredient for pyramid building was the availability of human labour and during the annual flooding of the Nile Valley when it was impossible to farm the land, the Egyptian peasants were conscripted to carry heavy blocks of stone for hundreds of miles into the desert valleys. The scale of these operations was incredible; even with a substantial labour force at the king's disposal, each pyramid took up to twenty years to complete.

As architectural styles evolved, so the pyramid designs became even more stunning. The largest and most famous of them all, the Great Pyramid of Giza, was commissioned by Sneferu's son, King Khufu, and completed by 2560 BC. Such was the scale of the building that there was room for two wooden ships next to the royal burial chamber so the king would be able to sail across the heavens to rejoin the gods. The Great Pyramid is the only surviving member of the Seven Wonders of the World, later selected by classical Greeks, and serves as a vivid reminder of the extravagance of the Egyptian kings. Khufu's son, Khafra, continued in the same vein by constructing another majestic pyramid which was guarded by a colossal statue of a lion with a human head, known as the Great Sphinx. The intention was for the Sphinx to protect the king and ensure his smooth passage to the afterlife.

Subjects of the king could also be granted eternal life if they were buried in close proximity to their master and it was therefore common for rows of tombs to spring up around the pyramids. Unlike the king, these subjects would not expect to ascend to the heavens; instead their souls would continue to exist in the place where they were laid to rest, eternally protected by their divine ruler. To increase their chances of everlasting life, they would fill their tombs with statues and images to remind the soul of the life once lived. After the tomb had been sealed, the artefacts were believed to come to life and keep the soul entertained forever. The souls that were not protected by the king would be destined to float for eternity in the liquid chaos that surrounded the world.

This unwavering and fear-provoking belief in the afterlife was founded on the principle that everyone had both a soul and a vital force, known as the *ba* and *ka*. The *ba* was the unique personality of each individual that took flight from the body at the point of death, while the *ka* was the life force that every person possessed, which had to be constantly energised with food and drink. If the proper funeral rites were carried out, the two elements would unite to form the *akh,* which enabled the continuation of life. Also of significance was the *ren,* which was the name of each person. The Egyptians believed that as long as an individual's name was still written and spoken after death, the *akh* would be immortal. This encouraged each king to take several names, the most important being the Horus name, which affirmed his role as the divine king of Egypt. For instance, King Djoser's Horus name was Netjerikhet, meaning 'The most sacred one'. Djoser and his successors obsessively inscribed their names upon statues and monuments in the hope that their existence would be preserved forever.

Absorbed by their fanatical religious beliefs, the Egyptian people were extremely closed to outsiders, regarding them as inferior and unworthy beings. With every successful military campaign, the king's indisputable superiority was reaffirmed and the Old Kingdom rulers were certainly keen to extend the country's borders and reap the economic rewards. The most convenient target was the region of Nubia, immediately south of Upper Egypt. The primary aim of the Nubian campaigns was to control the local trade routes, particularly the desert oases, a strategy which often resulted in clashes between Egyptian soldiers and enemy tribes. Once the Nubian chiefs had been forced into submission, prisoners, cattle and goods such as ebony and ivory were shipped downstream.

A popular destination for trading ventures was the mysterious land of Punt, probably located in the Horn of Africa on the shores of the Red Sea. The treasures of Punt, including gold, myrrh and incense, were highly sought-after by the Egyptian nobility and many kings chose to exploit the region at some point in their reign. At the same time, mining expeditions were established in the eastern Sinai Desert, aided by the conscription of Nubian and Asiatic slaves, which produced large quantities of copper and turquoise that were transported back to the royal palace. Needless to say, Egypt was considerably more organised and powerful than any of its neighbours and as long there was harmony at home, the opportunity to exploit the riches of foreign lands proved to be a relatively easy task.

Unfortunately for the Egyptian monarchy, these favourable conditions disappeared during the Sixth Dynasty, when internal problems began to destabilise the smooth functioning of the state. A conspiracy against the long serving King Pepi was orchestrated by one of his own queens and although the plot ultimately failed, it suddenly became apparent that the kingship was not as impregnable as it had once seemed. This provided encouragement to some of the more ambitious provincial nomarchs, who were becoming increasingly autonomous, and during the reign of King Pepi II they decided to assemble their own armies and ships. Pepi and his successors were unable to appease the situation and some nomarchs began to claim it was *they* who were the legitimate heirs to the throne.

By 2200 BC the Old Kingdom had splintered into rival blocs, each headed by a wealthy nomarch. With no cohesion between them to properly execute foreign policy, the desert mines were abandoned, trade expeditions were halted and Nubia was left to its own devices, eventually uniting under an indigenous ruler in the city of Kerma. More worryingly, Asiatic tribes from the eastern desert began to encroach upon Egyptian territory and were able to seize much of the delta. The royal line continued in Memphis under the Seventh and Eighth dynasties, but the territory controlled by the king was restricted to the immediate area around the capital city.

The shift in power may seem sudden and dramatic, but was actually the result of ill-conceived policies that slowly but surely undermined the king's authority. The gradual distribution of riches and powers to the provinces encouraged a kind of feudal system, whereby the nomarchs mobilised labour on behalf of the king in exchange for controlling vast local estates. The king was also obliged to provide tombs and funerary gifts to the nomarchs as rewards for their service. This steady transfer of wealth enriched the local estates, while impoverishing the royal palace, and as the king's power began to diminish, so his aura disintegrated. The situation was worsened by climatic changes that frequently resulted in drought and famine. The remit of the king was to protect the people under the pretext of divine rule, but by the end of the Sixth Dynasty this protection could no longer be guaranteed and the king's mandate was lost. Fragmented and dispirited, the Old Kingdom frittered away to a disappointing end, belying the dazzling monuments that have preserved the glory of its name.

VIII

The first intermediate period witnessed a significant cultural regression, with a notable deterioration in the quality of art and an abrupt end to monumental building projects. Yet there was some respite for the townsmen and villagers as they were able to devote more time to worshipping their local gods and were relieved from the burdens of forced labour and armed service. The country was divided again, but the two regions of Lower and Upper Egypt re-organised themselves and gradually recovered from the food shortages that had hampered them towards the end of the Old Kingdom. Centres of power were established at Herakleopolis in Lower Egypt, where the Ninth and Tenth dynasties were formed, and in Thebes in Upper Egypt, where the Eleventh dynasty co-existed with those in the north. For just over a century, these two independent kingdoms competed with each other, vying for control of the country.

At first it was the kings of Herakleopolis who seized the initiative, when King Kheti ascended the throne in c.2160 BC and claimed direct decent from the rulers of the Old Kingdom. Order was restored throughout the delta and Kheti's realm was extended as far south as Abydos, where an uneasy border with Upper Egypt was established. In the delta, the Asiatics were expelled and the eastern borders fortified, while new canals were constructed and trade routes with Syria and Palestine reopened. The Herakleopolitan leaders were clearly making progress but they still lacked the absolute power of their predecessors and were heavily reliant upon the support of the provincial nobles. This continued to be a source of weakness for the Herakleopolitan dynasties and they soon found themselves at the mercy of their Theban adversaries.

The first leader to unite the nomes of Upper Egypt was Mentuhotep, although it was his successor, Intef, who achieved the first military successes against the north. Having won the respect of the other nomarchs, Intef assumed the title 'Great Overlord of Upper Egypt' and extended his realm to the city of Elephantine, near the Nubian border. His son and successor, Intef II, assumed the Horus name 'Son of Ra'; a direct assertion of divine descent and a deliberate provocation to the rival dynasties in the north. In c.2100 BC, Intef and his northern counterpart, Kheti III, led their armies to central Egypt for a series of battles that would decide the destiny of the land. Intef struck the first blow, seizing the city of Abydos, before advancing north to the town of Asyut. After both sides suffered the death of their kings, it was the new Theban ruler, Mentuhotep II, who made the decisive breakthrough when he launched a successful assault on the town. With the Theban army in the ascendancy, many of the central nomes switched their allegiance and granted Mentuhotep a clear passage to Herakleopolis, enabling him to march proudly down the Nile, seal the reunification of Egypt and found the Middle Kingdom under the leadership of Thebes.

For the rest of his years, Mentuhotep commissioned various building projects and generally restored order and unity to the country. The king resided in Thebes, but re-established the position of Chancellor of Lower Egypt to keep the northern nomarchs in check. Indeed, in his determination not to repeat the mistakes of his predecessors, Mentuhotep paid particular attention to the activities of the nomarchs throughout the country, punishing those who had supported the Herakleopolitan cause and pursuing the remaining dissidents into the desert to prevent them from mobilising a rebel force against his rule. Even the nomarchs from Upper Egypt were monitored closely by trusted Theban officials to ensure that their powers did not become excessive.

Despite a degree of passive resistance from the most influential nomarchs, some of whom continued to control their own private armies, the authority of the king was by and large accepted across the land. Mentuhotep was soon able to launch new campaigns beyond Egypt's borders, marching west into Libya and then east into the Sinai Desert to ward off hostile nomads, while his son, Mentuhotep III, returned to the land of Punt to seek its treasures once more. It was not long before the hardships of the intermediate period and the bitter civil war was forgotten; the Middle Kingdom heralded a period of recovery in which the voices of dissent were emphatically silenced.

The Eleventh Dynasty came to an end with the death of King Mentuhotep IV, enabling his vizier, Amenemhat, to succeed him in 1985 BC. The accession of a vizier was unprecedented and may have been the upshot of Amenemhat's alleged observance of two miracles while on a quarrying expedition for his master: the birth of a new born gazelle on the stone which had been chosen for the king's sarcophagus and a storm that revealed a well in the desert, completely full of water. Some believe that the priesthood interpreted these events as a sign from the gods that Amenemhat should become king. Alternative theories attest that Amenemhat murdered Mentuhotep or simply that he ascended the throne because the king lacked a male heir. Whatever the circumstances of his accession, the new ruler made his mark by initiating a theological modification that was adhered to by Egyptian kings throughout the Middle and New Kingdoms. The hidden god Amun was the favoured deity of the Theban priesthood and nobles, deriving from the cosmology of Hermopolis. In order to elevate Amun to the head of the pantheon, the Thebans combined his name with the sun god, creating the syncretic deity: Amun-Ra.

Despite the prominence of Amun-Ra, this was not a move towards monotheism and the other gods continued to be worshipped with as much intensity as ever. By the time of the Middle Kingdom it was widely believed that all Egyptians could gain a place in the afterlife and that a judgement would take place in a court of the gods, presided over by Osiris. If the verdict was favourable, the deceased would be allowed to join the blessed in the eternal kingdom of the dead. If not, he would be consumed by a terrifying monster that was part crocodile, part hippopotamus and part lion. Also inspired by the cult of Osiris, the practice of mummification became established in this period, particularly with regards to the king's burial. The intention was to purify and protect the body by removing all internal organs, stuffing it with scented material, bandaging the corpse and covering the face with a mask, often made of gold. This practice continued into the New Kingdom and became an essential part of royal burials.

With a united and stable realm behind him, Amenemhat felt bold enough to move away from Thebes and established a new capital at Itjtawy in central Egypt. New expeditions were undertaken in Nubia and the Sinai Desert as the exploitative methods of the Old Kingdom recommenced. King Senusret succeeded Amenemhat and successfully conquered Lower Nubia before establishing Egyptian rule over the Kingdom of Kush in Upper Nubia. He also seized control of the oases in Libya, conducted a further expedition to Punt, resumed the extensive gold mining in the eastern deserts and extended commercial trade with merchants in Syria and Palestine. Senusret certainly showed no mercy to those who stood in his way, describing himself as 'the throat-slitter of Asia'.

Indeed, the Egyptian kings did not take kindly to resistance, as the people of Lower Nubia discovered when King Senusret III launched successive wars against them, killing thousands of men and enslaving their women and children. Fortresses were set up at intervals along the border, sailing down the Nile was prohibited and the Nubians were rigorously controlled by the military. The Egyptian people were ruled with a firm hand as well; conscription ensured that both military and labour forces were always adequately manned, while anyone who tried to avoid service was punished together with the rest of his family and sent to work in the most inhospitable mines with the Nubian and Asiatic slaves.

By the time King Amenemhat III succeeded to the throne in 1831 BC, Egypt was respected and feared from Kerma to northern Syria. Amenemhat ruled for nearly fifty years and it was during this period that the cultural and economic peak of the Middle Kingdom was reached. Many temples were built and there was a long period of peace, in which rebellions were few and far between. Valuable minerals such as gold, silver and turquoise flooded into the country from miles around and in many ways this period was unsurpassed by any other in the history of Egyptian civilization, such was the ease in which its culture and religion could flourish. With the kingdom at the height of its powers, the Egyptian people must have felt more secure than ever.

Unfortunately there were problems looming on the horizon, initially because of a succession crisis. King Amenemhat IV died in 1777 BC without a male heir, leading to the coronation of the first female ruler of Egypt, Queen Sobekneferu, who may have been the king's sister. When she died less than four years later, the stability and authority of the state, exemplified by the long reign of Amenemhat III, were visibly waning. The ephemeral kings of the Thirteenth Dynasty attempted to arrest the situation and foreign expeditions continued unabated in a public demonstration of monarchical power, but their authority was undermined when low water levels in the Nile led to crop failures and severely weakened the economy. Confronted with less vigilant controls than usual, Asiatic tribes began to seize the copper mines in the Sinai Desert and probably sensed the unease that was emanating from the royal palace. As the Egyptian army marched northwards, it was forced to abandon the southern fortresses, enabling Lower Nubia to regain its independence and reunite with the Kingdom of Kush.

The focus shifted to the preservation of royal authority in the delta, but it was here that another threat made itself known. The Egyptians had conventionally labelled all foreign leaders *Hyksos,* meaning 'chiefs of foreign lands', but over time the term came to be used for all members of the Asiatic tribes. Ironically, the vibrant policy-making of King Amenemhat III in the heyday of the Middle Kingdom led to many Hyksos moving to the Egyptian delta to assist in state building projects and as a result they steadily infiltrated Egyptian society. By the time of the Thirteenth Dynasty, the Hyksos comprised the majority in some parts of the delta and even founded their own capital at Avaris. To the astonishment of the Egyptian nobility, the delta was being usurped from within.

Over a period of several decades, the Egyptians steadily lost their grip on Lower Egypt as the Hyksos increased their numbers and influence. In the mid-Seventeenth Century BC, under the bold leadership of Salitis, the insurgents gained control of Memphis and founded the Fifteenth Dynasty; the first Egyptian dynasty to be ruled by foreigners. This was the beginning of the Second Intermediate Period; a century of divided rule that witnessed the comprehensive loss of the delta region to the Hyksos. Although the kings of the parallel Fourteenth Dynasty initially maintained a stable administration throughout the rest of the country, they were soon forced to retreat to Thebes.

The Middle Kingdom came to an end with devastating consequences for the notion of divine kingship. The Egyptians believed themselves to be the favoured people of the gods and obeyed their king as the supreme ruler of the universe, yet much of the country had been overrun by inferior barbarian tribes who worshipped false gods. If the king was really divine, how could he let this happen? Questions like this must have been at the forefront of every Egyptian's mind following the disastrous collapse of the Middle Kingdom. In fact, the ascendancy of the Hyksos heralded a new era in the history of Egypt; no longer could its leaders ignore the activities of independent tribes beyond the country's borders. Egypt had been forced to engage with the wider world, where foreign states had to be treated with respect and eventually, in some cases, on equal terms.

IX

Less than four hundred miles north of Egypt, on a tranquil island in the eastern Mediterranean, lay the roots of the classical world and the inspiration that would one day lead to the brilliance of Greece. The idyllic island of Crete was the birthplace of an enchanting civilization that has often been portrayed as an ancient utopia, far removed from the violent struggles of Mesopotamia and Egypt. There may have been some early cultural influences from these regions, but Cretan society developed so uniquely that credit must be given to the ingenuity and originality displayed by its mysterious island population. For good reason, they are now regarded as the founders of civilization in what would eventually be known as the continent of Europe.

Crete was accessible to adventurous seafaring peoples from the Near East and it seems likely that the first settlers came from this direction. Over three thousand years of Neolithic farm life followed, before a new era began to emerge after the coming of the Bronze Age at the end of the Fourth Millennium BC. Initially society progressed slowly, with various coastal towns and villages contentedly trading metals and crafts with each other and the neighbouring islands, but in the Second Millennium BC the erection of several great palaces invigorated the Cretan people. The most famous palace was built at Knossos in c.1900 BC, where the legendary King Minos was said to live. The term *Minoan*, later used to describe the people and culture of ancient Crete, derives from his name.

Whether or not Minos was a real historical figure is unknown, but classical Greek mythology paints a delightful picture of the remarkable events which supposedly took place during his lifetime.

Minos was said to have married Pasiphae, the daughter of the Sun. One day he was presented with a white bull by the god Poseidon, but rather than sacrificing it in the god's name, Minos decided to keep the gift for himself. In retribution, Poseidon caused Pasiphae to be seduced by the beast and they soon produced a grotesque offspring known as the Minotaur; a terrifying monster that was part man and part bull. The Minotaur was imprisoned in a great labyrinth at Knossos, devouring all who came his way.

At the time, Minos had a bitter rival by the name of King Aegeus of Athens and many Athenians were taken prisoner and sent to the labyrinth where they faced the relentless task of evading the Minotaur. Angered by these events, Theseus, the brave son of Aegeus, came to the labyrinth to kill the monster. While in Crete, Theseus fell in love with Ariadne, the daughter of Minos, who helped him navigate the labyrinth with a ball of string. The valiant Theseus made his way to the centre of the maze and slew the Minotaur once and for all, before leading the imprisoned Athenians to safety and fleeing the island with his beloved Ariadne. Before his journey to Crete, Theseus had told his father that if he survived the task, he would replace the black sails of his ship with white sails upon his return. However, he forgot to make the change and when Aegeus saw the black sails, he despairingly threw himself into the sea and drowned. It is from this tragic tale that the Aegean Sea takes its name.

Obviously the story of King Minos cannot be taken at face value and the early influence of Athens is anachronistic, but there is archaeological evidence of a labyrinth at Knossos and it was principally around this city that Minoan civilization began to thrive. Cretan agriculture, strongly supported by olive and vine cultivation, had improved considerably since Neolithic times and permitted a gradual rise in population. In due course, the increasingly healthy economic situation and availability of mass labour enabled the construction of majestic palaces in the cities of Phaistos, Malia, and most remarkably at Knossos, where the palace was flanked by the labyrinth and an expansive courtyard. Throughout Crete there were numerous independent clans and the most successful among them formed the ruling classes, including members of the royal family, nobility and priesthood.

In c.1700 BC the palaces were either destroyed or severely damaged by a large earthquake that rocked the island, but the Minoans were unperturbed and built new palaces that were even more impressive than those which preceded them. At Knossos the labyrinth was expanded to become one of the most incredible constructions of the ancient world, decorated lavishly with sacred images and filled with hundreds of hidden corridors and chambers. Beautiful works of art and colourful frescos adorned the palaces, while craft workshops in and around the temples produced a variety of goods which were either offered to the priesthood or exported abroad. High quality Cretan exports included elaborate cloths, bronze figurines, decorated pottery, jewellery and edible goods such as spices, olive oil and wine. These commodities were carried far and wide by Minoan merchants to destinations such as Egypt, Cyprus and developing city-states in Greece.

In return, the traders brought home raw materials such as timber and copper, as well as quantities of silver and gold that could be reworked into exquisite items by the Minoan craftsmen. Another essential import was tin, a metal which the Minoans needed to forge with copper to make bronze. This may have been obtained from as far as Spain or Britain. Yet the most intriguing relationship was between Crete and Egypt, with Egyptian vases reaching Cretan shores as distinctive Minoan artwork graced the tombs of nobles near Thebes. There may have been an Egyptian official in Knossos acting as a diplomat and overseeing trade relations and there are even suggestions that Minoan soldiers assisted the Egyptians in their battles against the Hyksos at the end of the Middle Kingdom. Although the nature and extent of this relationship may never be known, a fascinating degree of mutual respect seems to have emerged between these two very different civilizations.

By the Sixteenth Century BC, Minoan goods were heavily in demand throughout the Mediterranean and beyond, enabling the Cretan sailors to establish what can only be described as a trading empire. This development encouraged the foundation of colonial settlements from which the Minoan merchants could easily deal with their foreign counterparts. The majority of these were based on neighbouring islands, such as Melos and Rhodes, although the most prestigious was the colony of Miletus on the Anatolian coast. Mainland Greece was also influenced by Crete during this period and absorbed much of Minoan culture, although there is no evidence to suggest that any colonies were founded there.

Expansionism in the ancient world was usually enacted by military campaigns and the suppression of weaker states; however the remnants of Minoan civilization do not imply they were a warlike people, certainly not in comparison to their Near Eastern neighbours. Even the colonies appear to have been established by quiet infiltrations rather than aggressive invasions. Perhaps the rich and plentiful goods from Crete were welcomed and embraced by her less illustrious neighbours, precluding the need for a military presence. Indeed, there are no records in Crete of tyrannical leaders, divine kings or great warriors with pretentions to conquer vast lands and rule the known universe. Instead we are left with an impression of a peaceful civilization that had altogether different priorities.

The reason for the lack of ambition in comparison to Mesopotamia or Egypt may lie in the subdued nature of Cretan kingship. There are indications that the king did not reside in the palaces after all and that he was in effect a secular ruler with limited powers, inferior to the priests and priestesses who were the central characters of the island. In fact the palaces may actually have been temples where the public came to worship their gods and donate gifts. The king is rarely mentioned in palace records, although it appears that he had at least some kind of ceremonial role in religious and military affairs.

In contrast, the high profile priesthood initiated important religious rituals and probably set taxes throughout the land. As in Egypt and Mesopotamia, Minoan religion was polytheistic: they believed in the existence of multiple gods and goddesses. The main deity was the goddess Potnia, affectionately known as 'The Lady'. Other goddesses included the Mistress of Wild Animals, the Goddess of Fertility and the Snake Goddess of the underworld; although some may have been aspects of Potnia, whom they regarded as an ever-changing spirit of nature. The Minoans passionately embraced the natural world, as evidenced by the vast array of animals in their colourful frescos and intricate pottery engravings.

The Cretan goddesses were accompanied by their male companions, the most important of whom was Poteidan, who was to evolve into the great Poseidon of Greece. However the ascendancy of the female deities persisted and the priestesses dominated religious rites. It is unclear whether this amounted to genuine power or was purely symbolic to reflect the superior role of the goddesses, but either way the rituals must have been amazing spectacles, with the priestesses wearing specially made costumes and performing sacred dances before their captivated audiences. They also participated in the rite of bull-leaping, an event that often took place in the centre of the labyrinth at Knossos and required teams of dancers to perform somersaults and acrobatic jumps over a bull, which represented the god Poteidan. The whole experience was enhanced by alcohol and opium, creating a religious euphoria which led the Minoans to believe they were no longer observing the priestesses, but the goddesses themselves.

Completely immersed in religion and the vitality of their cultural activities, the Minoans appear to have been contented and settled in their peaceful way of life. They have been commonly portrayed as beautiful and natural people who loved art, wildlife, festivals and sports, living harmoniously on their utopian island, undisturbed by the invasions and upheavals of the Near East. Much emphasis was placed on physical appearance; the women were bare-chested with long wavy black hair, beautified with make-up, jewels and fabrics, while the men were muscular, tanned and also thinly dressed. Society was peaceful and inspired by theocratic rule that was overseen by elegant and glamorous priestesses. Farms and villages were scattered throughout the countryside, surrounded by vineyards and olive groves that were warmed by the rays of the Mediterranean sun. The Minoans happily danced and played, decorated their buildings and drank their wine, safe in the knowledge that they were protected by the sea from the cruel outside world. If ever a society was verging on perfection, Minoan Crete seems to have been as close as one can imagine.

Yet we should not rule out a darker side of Crete that has been overshadowed by these impressions of devotion to nature and social harmony. For instance, there are indications of human sacrifice and ritual cannibalism, even involving children. The Minoans also possessed bronze armour and weaponry, and cannot have been untrained in warfare. The dangerous presence of pirates and aggressive states in all directions would have made some form of self defence a necessity, even if the Minoans were not seeking to invade and rule foreign lands themselves. Nevertheless, the cities in Crete were unfortified and seem to have remained on friendly terms with each other. It does seem as though the people of Crete were adverse to war in a principled fashion that their neighbours and contemporaries would never have contemplated. Such was the mystical aura surrounding the priestesses that any violation of the natural order would perhaps have seemed like an affront to the gods and goddesses.

Minoan culture flourished unimpeded for decades, but in the late Sixteenth Century BC it came to an abrupt and dramatic end.

A huge volcanic eruption on the nearby island of Thera caused devastation throughout the Aegean and buried whole towns and cities under mountains of white ash. The enormity of the explosion must have been petrifying for the Minoan people who would have seen the sun blotted out by dark poisonous clouds. As terror spread across the land, the initial blast was probably followed by a succession of earthquakes and a tsunami, flooding the harbours and leaving the desperate Minoans to look to the heavens in despair. The fields were blackened and the vegetation ruined, the palaces were completely destroyed and the inhabitants of cities such as Phaistos and Malia were forced abandon their homes for good. Thousands must have perished in the wake of Thera.

For those who survived, the aftermath of the destruction would have been a horrific time to endure, probably arousing levels of desperation which led to violence and civil war. Many of the cities that survived the eruption were burned to the ground soon afterwards. It seems there was a general loss of faith as well, indicated by a reduction in the number of sanctuaries. Only Knossos showed any signs of recovery and from 1450 BC it stood virtually alone as a bastion of Minoan civilization. Eventually the palace and labyrinth were restored and the remaining wealth of the island and its colonies was diverted to Knossos. The city presided over a centralised state that at least offered hope to the Cretan population.

The perseverance of Knossos may have been an achievement in adversity, but it is unlikely that the Minoans instigated the revival themselves. Instead it seems that Greeks from the mainland, unaffected by the eruption, sailed across the Aegean, past the sunken ships of the Minoan sailors, and imposed themselves upon the struggling inhabitants. Whether this was achieved by peaceful or forceful means is unknown, but the altered style of Cretan artwork and the infiltration of Greek writing appear to confirm their presence. A semblance of normality was restored for several decades in Knossos and the city continued to trade across the Mediterranean, but the renaissance was ultimately short-lived. Further invaders from the mainland, perhaps from a rival city-state, ravaged Knossos and immersed the city in flames. The palace and labyrinth were left in tatters and never rebuilt again. Once and for all, Crete had been overpowered by Greece, and as new settlers arrived and old traditions gradually petered away, the beautiful Minoan civilization was at last consigned to history.

X

By the middle of the Second Millennium BC, the three quintessential civilizations of the Near East and eastern Mediterranean had been breached: Mesopotamia was left stunned by the Hittite invasion of Babylon, Egypt had been split in two by the encroaching Hyksos, and Crete had been rocked by the Thera eruption and finally overcome by Greek opportunism. Having wilfully exploited their neighbours for centuries, the enduring powers of Babylonia and Egypt were at last having to acknowledge new forces which had the ability to consistently challenge them militarily and compete for valuable land and resources. The dynamics of the ancient world were rapidly changing and the chief cause was the recent arrival of an energetic group of tribes known as the Indo-Europeans.

It is important to stress that the term *Indo-European* is purely linguistic, denoting speakers of various related languages, rather than a unified ethnic group. Even today, the majority of languages in Europe are classified as Indo-European, while variations are spoken worldwide, from India to the Americas. Yet for centuries it was the Semitic languages of Mesopotamia and the native Egyptian language of the Nile Valley that dominated the civilized world and the new arrivals must have seemed quite alien to the local inhabitants. Similarities among the various Indo-European languages indicate that at some stage at an unknown time in prehistory there was just one original language which later split into numerous branches. This language was probably spoken in a prehistoric Indo-European homeland, most likely located north of the Caucasus Mountains in what is now Russia and the Ukraine, perhaps straddling the northern shoreline of the Black Sea.

The existence and location of an original homeland is often disputed, with some historians supporting the older theory that the Indo-Europeans came from a region north of India. Yet such is the scarcity of information outside the Near East and Egypt during this period that the definitive origins of external populations may never be known. Wherever they came from, the Indo-European tribes unquestionably displayed similar characteristics to each other: they were all skilled in horsemanship and metal-working and developed the wheel from an early date. They were also pastoralists and it was this need to find fresh pastures that led them to the Near East and beyond.

In the late Third and early Second Millennium BC, the Indo-Europeans began to settle on the fringes of Mesopotamia. The first to arrive were the Hittites, who settled in Anatolia, closely followed by another group who infiltrated the native Hurrian tribes in the foothills of the Taurus Mountains. Further east, in the Zagros Mountains, a separate branch mingled with another group of natives, known as the Kassites. Both the Hurrians and Kassites were profoundly affected by the migrations; neither had wielded much influence in Mesopotamia during the successive Sumerian, Akkadian and Babylonian hegemonies, but this all changed when the Indo-European warriors began to impose their own chieftains, deities and military culture. Important advantages were gained over neighbouring territories, particularly through the introduction of the horse and chariot, which led to the formation of trained cavalries with the capacity to overwhelm enemy infantrymen on the battlefield.

The Indo-European tribes continued to spread over vast distances, reaching Greece by 1800 BC and the Indus Valley soon afterwards. Over the next few centuries their impact would be immense: the Greeks inherited the Minoan sea-empire, the Hittites formed a powerful new kingdom in Anatolia and the Hurrians and Kassites zealously followed in their footsteps in Syria and

Mesopotamia. The young and enterprising Indo-European states soon established themselves as the dominant forces in the Near East; a feat which ultimately set them on a collision course with the mighty armies of Egypt.

XI

Over a thousand years before its famous classical era, ancient Greece was first civilized in the Bronze Age by an Indo-European tribe which later became known as the Mycenaeans, named after their greatest city, Mycenae. Much of the information we have on Mycenaean Greece derives from the epic poems of Homer, entitled *The Iliad* and *The Odyssey*. The poems were composed centuries later, probably in the Eighth Century BC, and they respectively describe the Greek campaign against the Anatolian city of Troy (*Ilion* in Greek) and the perilous homecoming of the hero Odysseus, who had been instrumental in the Greek victory. Although the poems were influenced by centuries of storytelling about immortal powers and mythical events, some aspects have since been supported by historical or archaeological evidence, particularly in respect of the legendary Trojan War. The Homeric poems seem destined to remain in a grey area between fiction and history, but there is no doubt that their dramatic depiction of the Mycenaean age was to have a monumental impact upon classical Greek civilization.

The land of Greece was largely unoccupied until the dawn of the Bronze Age, when the arrival of the plough enabled farmers from Anatolia to settle in both the expansive plains of the north and the hilly terrain of the south. For centuries the inhabitants traded peacefully with Crete and Anatolia from small towns and villages throughout the country. Then, in c.1800 BC, the cultural landscape began to change as the first speakers of an early form of Greek began to arrive in waves from the east, eventually forcing their way into Attica and the Peloponnese, before settling among the existing populations. These migrants were originally known as the Achaeans and although their exact path is unknown, they may have come directly from the fabled Indo-European homeland to the north of the Black Sea. As was typical of Indo-Europeans, they brought with them horses, chariots and a warlike heritage that resulted in the building of fortified castles upon elevated land, known as the *acropolis*. These settlements soon developed into cities, of which the most prestigious was Mycenae.

The divergent physical geography of Greece, with mountain ranges separating fertile plains, led to the permanence of independent kingdoms, most of which had their own harbour and fleet of ships. These conditions made it difficult to unite the whole country, although language, religion and architectural styles were shared and it is likely that some kind of political federation existed under the auspices of Mycenae. Mycenaean Greece incorporated a sizeable area, including several diminutive kingdoms in the north, but these sites did not command the same economic power as those in the Peloponnese and it was the latter region that dominated from an early stage. In addition to Mycenae, other important cities of the Peloponnese included Tiryns, Argos and Pylos. Meanwhile, in the eastern peninsula of Attica lay the city of Athens; a famous name whose golden age was yet to come.

It is striking that Mycenaean Greece has not left behind a vast array of statues or literary references to kings. As in Crete, it may have been that the palaces were actually temples, particularly as offerings to the gods were frequently sent to them by dutiful members of the public. The priests and priestesses led religious ceremonies in a similar manner to their counterparts in Crete and it is conceivable that they held equivalent positions of power. Yet despite the paucity of royal remnants, it is generally assumed that the leaders of Mycenaean Greece operated as warrior-kings in true Indo-European fashion.

The king was known in Greek as the *wanax*; a title which referred to the ruler of each independent city, rather than a centralised monarch who reigned across the entire land. In each city, the *wanax* was supported by the chief of the army and a group of elites who resided in large country estates and controlled both domestic and foreign policy, while benefiting from the thriving trade with the Near East and Mediterranean islands. They were served by palace scribes, merchants and free citizens, the *damos*, who mainly resided in the countryside where they farmed the land and transported produce to the cities. At the bottom of the social hierarchy were the slaves who had been captured from the Aegean islands and the Anatolian coast. Slave families were usually separated immediately, with the women and children made to work on the farms while the men were either forced to build the great citadels or executed to prevent future revolts.

Another similarity to Crete was the religious hysteria that gripped the population. Spiritual festivals and euphoric dancing were commonplace, while the Minoan use of alcohol and opium to enhance the religious experience seems to have been imported as well. The Minoan gods and goddesses appear to have evolved into the Mycenaean pantheon in a fusion with archaic Indo-European beliefs. The most noteworthy import from Crete was Poteidan, who evolved into Poseidon, the chief god of Mycenaean Greece. Poseidon was later transcended by his brother, Zeus, who is named as the king of the gods in the Homeric poems. Although Zeus was one of several classical gods to be revered by the Mycenaeans, the timing of his rise to prominence is uncertain; Homer lived hundreds of years later than the period he describes and the pantheon of his poems may in fact be a misleading reflection of Mycenaean religion. Either way, there is no question that the Bronze Age Greeks were extremely pious. Setting the tone for their descendants, they viewed all acts on Earth to be the will of the gods and firmly believed the fate of mankind was preordained by their immortal superiors.

Moulded by war and religion, the Mycenaeans had an intense obsession with death and dedicated a great deal of time to funeral practices, only surpassed by the meticulous Egyptians. The gigantic *tholos* (beehive) tombs at Mycenae were built for the king and were the focal point of an elaborate ceremony where the deceased was laid down in his robes upon a carpet of gold and buried alongside his family and possessions. A ritual service performed by the priesthood would often include the slaughter of horses and rams before the animals were cooked and eaten within the tomb. There even appear to have been occasional human sacrifices. Homer alludes to this practice in *The Iliad* where he describes King Agamemnon's agreement to sacrifice his daughter, Iphigenia, to appease the goddess Artemis.

Religion shaped the attitudes of the early Greeks, but this did not prevent them from craving wealth and luxury. For many years Greece remained in the shadows of the distinguished Minoan civilization in Crete and it was not until the eruption of Thera, in the late Sixteenth Century BC, that the Mycenaeans were able to exert their authority over the Mediterranean and reap the rewards. Aside from occupying Knossos itself, they wasted little time in exploiting the Minoan sea-empire, while they also acquired knowledge from their neighbours in the fields of art, sculpture, writing and economic administration. The Mycenaeans were truly absorbed by Minoan culture, perhaps because their Indo-European roots were centred on a warrior-elite and lacked the subtleties and creative achievements of Crete. It was not long before splendid palaces modelled on Knossos were erected in the Greek cities, with wall-paintings and frescoes shamelessly imitating the Minoan style.

By the Fourteenth Century BC, the Mycenaeans dominated the Mediterranean. Minoan colonies such as Rhodes and Miletus were consolidated and expanded, while new settlements were established in Cyprus, Italy and Sardinia. As time went by, more and more Mycenaean sites were founded throughout the Aegean islands and the Asiatic coast. The Minoan trading system was enthusiastically adopted and the Mycenaeans eagerly imported tin, copper and ivory from the Near East, supplemented by exotic materials such as amber from the barbaric regions of Europe. A century later, they had assumed enough importance to make diplomatic contact with Egypt. They also imported gold from Nubia and frequently traded with Troy, the most prestigious city in north-western Anatolia.

While the temptation to inherit the riches of the Minoan trading empire must have been irresistible, Mycenaean trading activity was actually born from necessity, as unlike the rich and fertile river valleys of Babylonia and Egypt, Greece was perilously deprived of its own natural resources. The Mycenaeans overcame this predicament by selling many of the slaves who had been captured from the Aegean or Anatolia, while they also copied the Minoan practice of exporting wool to the colder regions of Europe. The increasing number of riches displayed by the Mycenaeans in their palaces and tombs was a clear measure of their commercial success, with extravagant items including boar-tusk helmets and amber necklaces. Such an accumulation of wealth was extraordinary, particularly within a decentralised political structure which enabled various self-governing cities to pursue their own objectives. In order to serve the common interest, it is likely there would have been some kind of code of etiquette observed by the city-states, perhaps administered by a loose federation at Mycenae, to ensure that competition between the Greek cities did not have an adverse effect on foreign trade.

Although their trading prowess is beyond dispute, it must be emphasised that the political and military power of the Mycenaeans was never akin to the great forces of Egypt, Babylonia, or even the emerging Hittites. The scale of Mycenaean trade was certainly acknowledged by the great powers of the region, but even this had only been possible following the simultaneous struggles in Egypt, Mesopotamia and Crete. The rulers of the Mycenaean city-states were not equipped, or inclined, to conquer land away from the Mediterranean sphere and were content to take advantage of the trading opportunities that had been presented to them.

XII

Further to the east, in the heart of central Anatolia, another group of Indo-European settlers took a more aggressive approach than their early Greek contemporaries. Although they have never inspired the minds of future generations like the Egyptians, Babylonians or Mycenaeans, the tribe that came to be known as the Hittites gained a reputation as formidable warriors, consistently excelling in the battlefield and eventually posing a genuine threat to the established powers of the ancient world. Relentlessly driven forward by ruthless and bloodthirsty kings, the nascent Hittite kingdom expanded rapidly, invoking fear and envy throughout the Near East and beyond.

The land of Anatolia, a fertile region comprising most of modern-day Turkey, was inhabited deep into Neolithic times and boasted the ground-breaking settlement of Catal Huyuk, which produced some of the most advanced pottery in the prehistoric world. Following the arrival of the Bronze Age and the spread of culture and innovative ideas from southern Mesopotamia, a recognisable form of civilization was attained towards the end of the Third Millennium BC through the emergence of city-states including Alaca Huyuk in the north and Troy on the north-western coast. Having established control over local food production and merchant trade, the leaders of each city-state set up residence in their own fortified castles and revelled in the flourishing metal trade of the period.

Unfortunately for them, the dynamics of the region changed in c.2100 BC, when three independent Indo-European tribes invaded from the north, probably via the passes of the Caucasus Mountains. The first to arrive were the Luwians and, riding upon their armoured horses, they quickly spread across the land, occupying much of south-western Anatolia and leaving a long trail of destruction in their wake. The Luwian language soon became widespread as the newcomers imposed their customs and way of life upon the native inhabitants. They were followed by the Palaites in the north and the Nesites in the central region, both of whom also came with the intention of staying. As the Nesites mixed with the native Hattian people, it was here in central Anatolia that the Hittite language began to evolve.

The wealth of the first Anatolian city-states was attributable to the metal trade with Mesopotamia and the Indo-European settlers continued this practice, taking advantage of Assyrian trading colonies which were conveniently located between the two regions. The Anatolians exported gold, silver and copper in exchange for large quantities of tin, which they needed to make bronze. However, in the Eighteenth Century BC, owing to Hurrian interference and the presence of the Babylonian army in Assyria, the colonies were disbanded. Their disappearance was disastrous for the Anatolians, who subsequently had to seek alternative routes along the Euphrates, dangerously close to the realm of Babylon.

During the final years of the Assyrian trading colonies, the nearby city of Kussara rose to prominence in eastern Anatolia. The first known ruler of the city, Pithanas, extended his domain by overcoming the neighbouring city of Kanesh, before his son and successor, Anittas, seized the city of Hattusas in the central region. By 1750 BC, Anittas ruled over a sizeable area, in which the Hittite language had become prevalent. Initially these successes appeared inconsequential, as soon after his death the royal palace at Kanesh was destroyed by invaders from the north, summarily ending any hopes of a lasting empire. Literacy disappeared in the region as well and because they no longer had a trade outlet to the Assyrian merchants, Anatolian civilization began to contract and decline. However an important legacy had been left behind: Anittas had given ambitious Hittites a tradition to aspire to and those with pretentions for kingship improved their credentials by claiming descent from the legendary king.

A century later, a new kingdom was established in Kussara by an influential warlord named Labarnas. Sometime after 1650 BC, his son, Labarnas II, followed in the footsteps of Anittas by defeating his rivals and expanding the kingdom to include the city of Hattusas. The city was strategically located on high ground, providing a suitably secure stronghold for a capital city. To reflect its importance, the king changed his name to Hattusilis and claimed dominion over the entire central region of Anatolia, which henceforth became known as Hatti. A palace was built in Hattusas as the king sought to consolidate his rule. This time the Hittites were to show greater staying power and it was under Hattusilis that they first became recognised outside Anatolia as a major force to be reckoned with.

Life inside Hatti would have been similar to other parts of Anatolia, with each village governed by a council of elders, represented by the fathers of the leading families. These men controlled their own households and had the power to choose husbands for their daughters or, curiously, to give away their sons to other families who had lost their own in battle. As was customary in the ancient world, religion, sacrifice and obedience to the king underpinned society. To stave off crises such as disease or famine, priests and priestesses performed magic rituals to protect those affected, often involving the sacrifice of dogs. More conventionally, the bones of other animals such as horses and cattle were laid to rest with their deceased masters in order to serve them in the afterlife. There were no lavish tombs comparable to Egypt and the Hittites often preferred to be cremated; a custom shared by many of their contemporaries in Anatolia and Mycenaean Greece.

The people of Hatti were relatively unsophisticated compared to their neighbours and produced little artwork or sculpture of note. Indeed, their limited achievements have often led to them being depicted as uncouth barbarians. Yet although the Hittites did not emulate the Mesopotamians or Egyptians in terms of grandeur and style, they were equally competent in the practice of state administration, having adopted cuneiform script from Syria and trained their own scribes in writing and economics. More worryingly for neighbouring states, their skilled cavalry gave them an advantage on the battlefield that they were particularly keen to demonstrate.

The quest for expansion was probably driven by the need for tin, which had been in short supply since the disappearance of the Assyrian colonies, while the existence of fertile farmland in Mesopotamia was a tantalising prospect. To achieve his objectives, Hattusilis knew he would have to venture towards the imposing kingdom of Babylon, but rather than marching recklessly down the Euphrates, he first elected to extend Hittite influence and acquire valuable resources by conquering smaller city-states in northern Syria. Some of the weaker cities were soon captured, but the stronghold of Aleppo proved to be a much trickier proposition and Hattusilis was left frustrated by its resistance.

With his mission incomplete, the king was called back to Hatti to deal with an opportunistic invasion by the Luwians. Without access to a coastline, the Hittites had to defend against enemies on all sides, including the Gasga tribes in the north, the Hurrians in the east and the Luwians in the west. Hattusilis defeated the Luwians in battle and then overcame a Hurrian attack in the east, enabling his army to advance to the fringes of the Euphrates Valley. However, despite returning to Syria, he was never able to defeat Aleppo and for this reason he began to lose the confidence of his closest supporters, with even his own sons turning against him. In his desperation to succeed, it seems that Hattusilis was killed in battle in 1620 BC as he continued to fight for control of the elusive Syrian city.

It might have been expected that the Hittites would retreat

inside their own borders following the king's death, but his grandson, Mursilis, was not about to let that happen. Realising that he needed reinforcements to overcome the Syrian army, Mursilis instigated an alliance with the fledgling Kassite kingdom of Hana. The Hittite-Kassite alliance proved too strong for Aleppo and Mursilis triumphed, gaining access to new fertile land and much of the Euphrates trade route. By the Sixteenth Century BC, the situation in Mesopotamia had become more favourable for the Hittites, principally because Babylon was suffering from the loss of its territories in Sumer and the effects of a crippling food crisis. Taking advantage of this state of affairs, in 1595 BC Mursilis audaciously led the Hittite army to the gates of Babylon and stormed the famous city, stripped it of its treasures, including the holy statue of Marduk, and marched back up the Euphrates in a state of jubilation.

The victory over Babylon was an astonishing success but it also proved to be the peak of the Old Hittite Kingdom. Perhaps because the speed of their victory had taken them by surprise, the Hittites were not equipped to occupy Babylon on a permanent basis and many of the city's treasures were left to their Kassite allies in Hana. Soon afterwards, Mursilis was brutally murdered by his jealous brother-in-law, plunging the kingdom into crisis. Unable to recover their composure, the Hittites were left to rue what might have been as the Hurrians and Luwians took back their former territories and forced Hatti to retreat to its original borders in central Anatolia. The raid of Babylon may not have resulted in a lasting Hittite Empire, but it certainly gave them a taste for greater things. In due course, a new Hittite kingdom would rise to become one of the most powerful states in the ancient world.

XIII

O riginating in the Zagros Mountains in the east, the native Kassites appear to have been infiltrated by another group of Indo-Europeans, before migrating west into Amorite-controlled Babylonia during the Seventeenth Century BC. Having established themselves in the region, they progressed from labourers to landowners, steadily growing in both numbers and influence. It was Hammurabi's son, Samsuiluna, who first identified the Kassites as a threat, ushering them away from Babylon to the settlement of Hana, where the first Kassite state was born. Much later, after the Hittite withdrawal from Babylon, the Kassites, led by King Agum, made the short journey down the Euphrates and seized the famous city for themselves.

Agum's first act was to appease the Babylonian people by recovering the statue of Marduk from the Hittites and returning it to the holy city. Continuing a strategy of pacification for the next four hundred years, the Kassites focused on promoting stability as the inhabitants recovered from the psychological effects of a long period of decline and the trauma of the Hittite invasion. In 1475 BC, the reunification of Babylonia was achieved when the breakaway state of Sealand was conquered by Prince Ulamburiash, brother of the Babylonian king, Kashtiliashu. The Kassites also had aspirations for restoring control of northern Mesopotamia, where they claimed Assyria as a Babylonian province, but the presence of the Hurrians prevented them from doing so.

They may not have covered themselves in glory, but the Kassite kings were exceptionally competent and pragmatic rulers who maintained the unified state of Babylonia for a much longer period than any of their predecessors, appeasing the southern separatists by paying regular attention to the Sumerian temples and judiciously maintaining law and order across the land. Similarly to the Amorites before them, they embraced Babylonian culture and favoured the continuation of old traditions rather than imposing their beliefs upon the existing population. Even the Kassite language remained secondary to Akkadian, the *lingua franca* of the Near East, which continued to be spoken by noblemen throughout Mesopotamia, Anatolia and Egypt.

Conservative and unspectacular, yet steadfast and enduring, the Kassites were exactly what Babylon needed to end the state of depression which followed the death of Hammurabi and they ensured that Babylonia recovered economically and regained its dignity and presence on the international stage. Their inability to reclaim Assyria was a constant source of frustration, but the Kassite kings were nonetheless able to converse with their counterparts in Egypt and Hatti as respectable statesmen. Long term peace was difficult to achieve in the ancient world and the Kassite period must have been a welcome relief for the exhausted citizens of southern Mesopotamia.

The Kassites had gone a long way from being insignificant nomads in the Zagros Mountains to ruling a grand and prosperous kingdom, and the same was true of the Hurrians, another tribe to be influenced by the wandering Indo-Europeans. Not a great deal is known about their background, but it is likely that they came from the Armenian highlands and gradually migrated south to the upper reaches of the Tigris and Euphrates. By the Sixteenth Century BC, the Hurrians had established a number of small kingdoms throughout northern Mesopotamia and Syria. Although the next sequence of events is vague, it seems that the Hurrian kings were usurped by a warrior class of Indo-Europeans which proceeded to rule over the indigenous population. The warlords introduced elements of their own language and several mysterious Aryan deities which were concurrently being worshipped in the Indus Valley by their Indo-European cousins. By 1500 BC, the overlords had integrated the Hurrian kingdoms into a single powerful state, known as Mitanni. The natives were trained in horsemanship and chariot warfare, giving them a perceptible military edge over many of their contemporaries.

The Kingdom of Mitanni was located in northern Mesopotamia, but at its zenith it extended as far as the borders of Babylonia and Hatti. The capital city, Washukanni, has never been found, although it is believed to have been located somewhere near the Khabur River in north-eastern Syria. From this location, the Mitannians initiated military affairs and controlled vassal states, mainly in the Levant. By the reign of King Paratarna in 1480 BC, the state had absorbed the largest Syrian cities and expanded in the east where it effectively converted Assyria into a Mitannian province. Covering the long stretch of territory from the Zagros Mountains to the Mediterranean, the Mitannians roamed freely across the land on their horses, controlling numerous settlements and vast areas of agricultural land.

In the first half of the Fifteenth Century BC, with the Hittites still recovering from the death of Mursilis and the Kassites preoccupied with keeping order in Babylonia, it was the kingdom of Mitanni and its highly trained Hurrian army that harboured the greatest ambitions. However, if the Mitannians thought they could maintain their almost effortless swagger across the Near East, they were soon in for a rude awakening. In the land of the Nile, the Egyptians were stirring once more and readying themselves to exert revenge against the Asiatic usurpers who had callously torn apart their beloved Middle Kingdom. The paths of Egypt and Mitanni were about to converge, with implications for scores of communities across the Near East.

XIV

For a hundred years after 1650 BC, the Hyksos dynasty continued to rule Lower Egypt from the city of Avaris, while their counterparts in Thebes grudgingly remained in Upper Egypt, impatiently waiting for an opportunity to repossess the delta and reunite the country. For the native Egyptians, living under foreign rule may not have been much different from before, as the Hyksos had already assimilated into Egyptian culture and respected its traditions and practices. Generally speaking, ancient tribes tended to appreciate the high cultural achievements of others and were disinclined to destroy the few outstanding civilizations they encountered.

The Hyksos made their mark on Egypt by introducing their own styles of pottery and architecture, and continued to worship their favoured goddess, Astarte, but made no attempt to alter or regulate Egyptian religious practices and ruled Lower Egypt through administrative structures that were already in place. Importantly for the future dynasties of Egypt, the Hyksos also introduced the harnessed horse, enabling the Egyptians to participate in chariot warfare for the first time. Yet the Hyksos failed to make full use of this innovation themselves and no attempts were made to conquer territory beyond Egypt's borders; instead they directed their efforts at generating additional wealth through trade with autonomous cities in the Levant and Cyprus.

The noblemen of Thebes had no intention of yielding to the kings of Avaris and a rival dynasty was soon established in the south of the country. The Hyksos nominally claimed Upper Egypt as a vassal state, but in practice the Theban kings maintained their independence across the south, from the city of Cusae in the central region to Elephantine on the Nubian border. During this period, travel along the Nile in either direction became extremely hazardous as stringent border controls were enforced by the opposing sides and cross-border goods were heavily taxed. The Hyksos overcame this predicament by opening a trade route to Nubia via oases in the western desert. This arrangement was welcomed by the Nubian leaders who were not endeared to Thebes, having been subjugated by its kings during both the Old and Middle Kingdoms, and were accordingly more disposed to siding with the Hyksos.

Had a permanent trade embargo been rigidly enforced against Thebes, the Nubians and Hyksos could perhaps have strangled the life out of Upper Egypt, which lacked the resources to compete with the affluence of the delta; however in reality there was little to stop independent Nubian merchants from exchanging goods across the border with their fellow traders from Thebes, despite the official policy. The hub of trading activity in Nubia was the southern city of Kerma, where the Thebans acquired gold from the local mines and recruited mercenaries for its growing army.

The enmity between Avaris and Thebes reached boiling point in the middle of the Sixteenth Century BC, following the death of the Theban leader, Seqenenre. It appears the king suffered a violent death in a skirmish with the Hyksos, probably from a blow to the head by an axe. The incident enraged his son, Kamose, who vowed to avenge his father's death and restore native Egyptian control of Lower Egypt. His closest advisors were wary of launching a hasty attack for fear of over-committing and losing their independence in Upper Egypt as well, but Kamose could not be deterred from his mission. As part of his preparations, he marched southwards in a bid to secure unrestricted access to the Nubian gold mines and after three years of fighting he reclaimed the prized fortress of Buhen on the Nubian stretch of the Nile, before reinforcing his army with a new wave of mercenaries from Kerma.

As Kamose led his fleet down the Nile, the Hyksos scrambled

to resist the approaching hordes. Their king, Apepi, hastily sent a message to the King of Kush to try and rekindle the alliance with Nubia, but Kamose intercepted the correspondence and ordered his soldiers to block the oasis trade route, isolating Apepi in the delta. The Thebans continued to make progress down the Nile and took the opportunity to seize a number of nomes in the central region and to devastate the countryside on route to the Hyksos capital. Yet in spite of the bold assertions of Kamose, the Theban army did not reach the delta and the anticipated siege of Avaris failed to materialise.

Kamose died from unknown causes in 1550 BC and was succeeded by his younger brother, Ahmose, who was still a child at the time. This necessitated a slight delay in proceedings, but as soon as he had acquired enough strength and authority to lead his people, Ahmose ordered his troops to march north to Heliopolis and then onwards to the eastern fortress of Tjaru to block the enemy escape route to the Near East. The Hyksos were effectively surrounded in Avaris. As they made their way to the capital, the Theban soldiers enthusiastically flung themselves into battle, slaughtering anyone and anything that stood in their way. Unable to withstand the attack, the incumbent Hyksos king, Khamudi, ordered his men to gather their valuables and take refuge with their wives and children behind the city walls. The ensuing blockade condemned the Hyksos to defeat and although Ahmose reluctantly sanctioned a mass evacuation, this was under the proviso that the Hyksos were to leave Egypt at once and never return. The beleaguered Asiatics agreed and fled for their lives across the Sinai Desert.

Egypt was reunited once more, but Ahmose was not content to rest upon his laurels. Following in the footsteps of the departing Hyksos, the triumphant king marched through the Levant, pillaging towns and cities that were further away than any Egyptian army had ventured before. He later campaigned in the south as well and reinforced Egyptian control over Nubia, creating an extended realm which formed the basis of the New Kingdom. In his final years, Ahmose began to rebuild the great cities of Lower Egypt, erecting new temples for the gods and replacing the palaces which had been constructed by the Hyksos. Special attention was paid to the temples of Amun, the patron god of Thebes, whose standing had been neglected by the dynasty at Avaris. A fascinating aspect of the building programme was the introduction of Minoan frescos in the Egyptian palaces and it even appears that Ahmose married a princess from the island. Sadly the special relationship between these two contrasting cultures was to be severed by the eruption of Thera a few decades later.

Egypt was to be more fortunate than her Mediterranean neighbour and following the death of Ahmose in 1525 BC, his eldest surviving son, Amenhotep, continued the revival. The campaigns in the Levant had developed trade routes which steadily increased the wealth of the state, enabling precious metals to be transferred to newly erected temples and dedicated to the gods. The temples of Amun received the most attention, although the whole country felt the benefits of peace and prosperity as Egypt returned to the economically stable position it had enjoyed during the Middle Kingdom. Amenhotep's reign passed peacefully and although the site of his tomb is disputed, he may have been the first of many Egyptian kings to be buried in a secluded valley near Thebes, later known as the Valley of the Kings.

His son and successor, Thutmose, held greater ambitions, and seeking further wealth and prestige, he embarked upon new campaigns in both Nubia and Syria. Despite some early successes, he was aware that the Kingdom of Mitanni was the dominant power in the Near East and took precautions to avoid a direct confrontation with the warriors from Washukanni who were numerically superior and possessed substantially more chariots than the Egyptians. His son, Thutmose II, opted to steer clear of the region altogether and focused instead on quashing a series of rebellions in Nubia. It would be left to a more courageous successor to stand up to the Mitannians.

When Thutmose II died in 1479 BC, his son, Thutmose III, was too young to rule and so the boy's aunt, Hatshepsut, became co-regent. Only the second woman to reign in Egypt following the brief rule of Sobekneferu three hundred years earlier, Hatshepsut initially pledged to look after the young king's affairs, but as the lure of power overcame her, she changed her mind and proclaimed herself the rightful Queen of Egypt. Never before had a woman held so much power and it is perhaps surprising that this state of affairs went relatively unchallenged in a world where women were regarded as possessions of men, yet Hatshepsut reigned for over twenty years and proved to be a proficient queen. She maintained public approval by undertaking a series of well publicised building projects and commissioning private tombs for her rich supporters, while she later completed a successful trading expedition to the land of Punt, obtaining countless treasures without the need for any lengthy military campaigns.

Hatshepsut died in 1458 BC, bringing to an end a period of rule which formally remained a co-regency. Thutmose III had by then reached the mature age of twenty-one and eagerly emerged from the shadow of his overbearing aunt. He had been permitted to take command of the army from adulthood and felt perfectly capable of ruling by himself. Intelligent, scholarly and artistic, Thutmose enjoyed botany, art and reading, particularly historical texts, and constructed several shrines to commemorate his ancestors. His creative interests were augmented by his military training and a burning desire for adventure which he was anxious to placate. If the Egyptian people already sensed they were living under the command of a truly exceptional ruler, the coming years were to confirm their convictions.

Thutmose quickly identified the divided regions of Syria and Palestine as land to be exploited and he wasted little time in preparing his soldiers for an armed expedition. His strategy to occupy, rather than simply raid, territories in the Near East was not only ground-breaking for an Egyptian ruler but also extremely daring, as many of the city-states in the region recognised the Kingdom of Mitanni as the prevailing imperial power. History had taught Thutmose that leniency towards the Asiatics could have devastating consequences for Egypt and he showed no hesitation in adopting a belligerent approach. He resolved to conquer as much foreign territory as possible and undertook no less than seventeen military campaigns to achieve his objective.

The Mitannians had been anticipating an Egyptian offensive since the earlier raids of Thutmose I and reacted by encouraging a defensive alliance of Syrian and Palestinian cities. The result was a fiercely contested battle outside the city of Megiddo, from which Thutmose emerged victorious. This proved to be a defining moment for the young king; the Egyptian army proceeded to pick off Mitannian vassal territories one by one, effectively conquering the region of Palestine and penetrating the Levant as far as the city of Ugarit on the west coast of Syria. Tribute was collected from each of the conquered cities and grain was transported back to the Nile Valley at regular intervals.

The Mitannians had ruefully observed the Egyptian advance without mobilising their army, unwilling to commit to a major war for the sake of their vassal states. However in 1447 BC the decision was taken out of their hands, as Thutmose commanded his men to cross the Euphrates, leading them directly into Mitannian territory in a brazen act that was effectively a declaration of war. The Egyptians had craftily assembled a fleet of ships by the Levantine coast which had been secretly transported overland to the Euphrates so that the army could cross the river at speed and without detection. The invasion took the Mitannians completely by surprise and several of their cities were sacked before anything resembling a defence force could be assembled.

Eventually the Mitannians roused themselves into battle and a bloody clash took place on the outskirts of Carchemish. With the wind in their sails and having had more time to prepare, the Egyptians gained the upper hand and forced the Mitannians to retreat. The Near East was stunned; suddenly the land of Egypt, detached from Mesopotamian politics throughout centuries of coexistence, had forced its way into the heart of region and defeated its leading power in battle. Tribute flooded back to Egypt from the Hittites, Babylonians and Assyrians, much to the annoyance of the Mitannian leadership, who reacted angrily by throwing their support behind local rebellions in Syria and Palestine against Egyptian rule. Finally the bitter rivals met again near the city of Qadesh in 1438 BC, where Thutmose recorded another victory over the Mitannian army, seizing a further three cities in the aftermath.

Had he chosen to do so, Thutmose could perhaps have led his troops even deeper into enemy territory and conquered the entire Mitannian Empire, but instead he decided to settle for the innumerable riches he had obtained and a truce with the Mitannians was concluded. Mitanni maintained its territory in the north, including large tracts of Assyria, while the Egyptians continued to collect tribute from the cities of Syria and Palestine. Having spent much of his life in the Near East, Thutmose had grown fond of the region and seems to have married as many as three Syrian princesses. After making the long journey home, he commissioned monuments and furnished the holy temples with gold. He even took the time to erase the inscriptions of Hatshepsut's name wherever it could be found, avenging his late aunt for depriving him of power in his younger days. After his death in 1425 BC, the name of Thutmose III was etched into Egyptian folklore and succeeding generations passed on tales about the legendary king who triumphantly crossed the Euphrates and defeated the Asiatic foe.

The successor to the throne, Amenhotep II, inherited a kingdom that was in a stronger position than ever before. He was obliged to preserve Egypt's new Asian territories and at first he did so confidently, leading his army into the Near East and quashing rebellions wherever they arose. The king was blessed with extraordinary physical strength and a fearless nature; in his spare time he led lion hunts on foot and during one military campaign was said to have defeated seven foreign princes singlehandedly. It therefore came as a shock to all concerned when he was suddenly faced with a major setback in Syria. The Mitannians had facilitated a revolt in the city of Carchemish, which Thutmose had seized from them a few years earlier. In response, the Egyptians marched into the region, expecting to nullify the rebellion and restore order, but were confronted by a significantly larger and better prepared Mitannian army. To the consternation of Amenhotep, the Egyptians were soundly defeated and forced to retreat, abandoning much of the land they had previously conquered.

It was becoming apparent that neither side had the ability to comprehensively defeat the other and the hostilities eventually ceased. Under Amenhotep's successor, Thutmose IV, an armistice was agreed and the Egyptian king began a stately tour of Mitanni, culminating in his marriage to the daughter of the Mitannian king, Artatama. This mutual change in attitude was probably hastened by the resurgence of the Hittites, who had regained their military strength and were threatening to expand their borders once again. Artatama and his military commanders wanted to avoid the prospect of war on two fronts, while peace provided a welcome respite for the war-weary Egyptians. Under the rule of King Amenhotep III, beginning in 1390 BC, Egypt improved its diplomatic relations with other states in the Near East as the Middle Kingdom mentality of superiority and isolation was slowly replaced by a pragmatic acceptance of the political situation. There was to be no turning back now; Egypt had made too many forays into Near Eastern affairs and had already become an important participant in the international arena.

Amenhotep married the daughters of the Mitannian and Babylonian kings and continued to enjoy the gifts bestowed upon him by weaker foreign kingdoms which were anxious to nurture friendly relations with Egypt. As trade flourished and tribute continued to pour into the country from its vassals, Amenhotep basked in another golden era of Egyptian civilization. For nearly forty years, he dedicated his time to extravagant building works, decorating the land with magnificent temples and shrines. He fathered at least six children with his main consort, Queen Tiye, and their unwavering companionship personified the solidity of the Egyptian state. Egypt's new outlook influenced religious ideas as well and for the first time it was widely accepted that foreign people were also the creations and subjects of Amun-Ra, the syncretic god who had first been invoked by the kings of the Middle Kingdom. Amenhotep was worshipped as the earthly incarnation of Amun-Ra and may have been deified during his lifetime. The Kingdom of Egypt remained peaceful, affluent and powerful throughout his reign; a state of affairs that was celebrated domestically and acknowledged by the envious civilizations of the Near East.

XV

By the Fourteenth Century BC, an intriguing international system had emerged, wherein the principal kingdoms had inadvertently created a balance of power. The proud nations of Egypt, Mitanni, Hatti and Babylonia, eventually joined by Assyria, frequently engaged in both diplomacy and political scheming as they endeavoured to preserve their status as great powers, increase their wealth and manoeuvre into a stronger position than their rivals. On the fringes of this system lay Mycenaean Greece, which had a degree of influence in the Near East, although to a lesser extent than the aforementioned states, while caught in the clutches of the great powers were the assorted city-states of the Levant, including the settlements of Jerusalem, Byblos and Damascus.

Despite the recent defeat to the Mitannians, Egypt was still regarded as the greatest of these powers at the turn of the century; a situation that was repeatedly emphasised by the Egyptians in their portrayal of the other kings as weak rulers who routinely begged and pleaded for Egypt to have mercy on them. Following the onset of peace with Mitanni, Egypt maintained control of its Palestinian vassal territories and lingered as a formidable threat to the major kingdoms in the Near East. Yet behind this vale of propaganda, the Egyptian king and his advisors were under no illusions as to the potential threat from their Asiatic neighbours, particularly with the painful defeat to Mitanni still fresh in their minds.

The main concern for Egypt was the re-emergence of the Hittites. Early suggestions of Hatti's return to dominance in Anatolia, following the conquests of Tudhaliyas II in the early Fourteenth Century BC, appeared to have been misplaced when the Hittite capital city, Hattusas, was sacked by local tribes, the foremost of which were the Gasga. This defeat coincided with the rise of Arzawa, a loose confederation of Luwian territories in south-west Anatolia which expanded eastwards and began to pursue separate diplomatic channels with the Egyptians. Regrettably for the Arzawan king, his claim to greatness was undermined by the failure of his civil servants to master Akkadian, still the language of diplomats and nobles, putting him in the embarrassing position of having to communicate with the Egyptian king in Hittite. As it happened, the Arzawan ascendancy did not last long and by the time King Suppululiumas ascended the Hittite throne in 1344 BC, the Arzawa lands had slipped back into the political wilderness, while the Hittites swiftly regained their territories in Anatolia and pressed on into northern Syria.

The Hittite revival was particularly worrying for the Mitannians, whose western territories were left dangerously exposed. Worse still, in the eastern half of the empire, Assyria was increasingly presenting itself as a sovereign state, despite its official subservience to the Mitannian king. Peace with Egypt was essential for Mitanni as it struggled to retain its status as a great power. Meanwhile, in Mesopotamia, the Kassite kings continued to preserve the unity of Babylonia, which had long since grown to include the former breakaway state of Sealand. Babylonian hegemony remained secure on both sides of the Tigris and all the way down to the Gulf. Supremacy over Assyria was continuously asserted by the Kassite kings as well, particularly in their correspondence with the Egyptians, but in reality they had precious little influence over their northern neighbours.

Diplomacy between the great powers was a protracted and arduous process, with envoys travelling for weeks or months at a time to deliver messages between them. Among the distinguished royal authors were Amenhotep of Egypt, his controversial successor, Akhenaten, Tushratta of Mitanni, Kadashman-Enlil and Burnaburiash of Babylon, Suppululiumas of Hatti and Assur-uballit of Assyria, all of whom wrote with considerable haughtiness, tempered every now and then by etiquette or political tact. Kings addressed each other as 'brothers' while leaders of the vassal states were referred to as their 'servants'. The collection of texts, engraved on clay tablets, was discovered at the archaeological site of Amarna in Egypt and the contents have since become known as the Amarna Letters.

Although the level of communication between rival kings was greater than ever before, the political situation was extremely delicate and the balance of power remained precarious, partly because paranoia and suspicion were so prevalent. In some exchanges, the kings complained about their 'brothers' not writing enough, for sending gifts which did not contain enough gold, or for appearing to favour other states. For instance, Burnaburiash protested vociferously to Amenhotep because he had recognised the Assyrian king, Assur-uballit, as an independent ruler. Indeed, Assur-uballit's carefully worded letters to the Egyptian king proved to be an effective device for improving Assyria's repute.

A common topic of conversation was royal marriage. Kings and queens in the ancient world had little desire for monogamous relationships and were content to use marriage as a necessary diplomatic tool. Princesses were often sent to marry foreign kings in order to strengthen the relationship between rival states, although there was one notable exception as the King of Egypt was forbidden from sending his daughters abroad by traditional law, much to the frustration of the other monarchs. Fortunately Egypt's vast gold reserves provided an adequate substitute for its lovely princesses. Diplomacy and trade were closely linked and the practice of exchanging royal gifts enabled the great kings to obtain all the exotic goods they desired, while the nobles acquired their own luxuries via the flourishing merchant trade. The relatively peaceful political climate was particularly beneficial to the Mycenaeans, whose trading empire was well placed to exploit the demand for elaborate gifts.

Unfortunately the effects of the new era were not positive for everyone. An unavoidable consequence of the increasing trade in luxury goods was the widening gap between the nobility and the rest of the populace. While friendships were forged between wealthy counterparts from different states, relations between the elites and masses within each kingdom became virtually non-existent. Poor families often chose to flee from their homes to escape a life of servitude, preferring to seek a nomadic existence in the deserts or mountains. Those who strayed across the borders of the other great kingdoms were forced to return home in an exchange of refugees; for although they had little sense of social responsibility, the kings still needed the common men to build their temples, work their mines and farm their land. With almost no prospect of improving their circumstances, the bulk of society was effectively enslaved to an exclusive club which flagrantly governed and manipulated the civilized world as they pleased.

XVI

Under the reign of King Amenhotep III, the Egyptian state appeared to be the epitome of stability; the kingdom was wealthy and territorially united, the king was respected at home and abroad and the all-powerful deity Amun-Ra was worshipped fervently across the land. Unfortunately this situation was about to change following the accession of arguably the most disruptive influence in Egypt's history and certainly one of the most controversial characters in the ancient world. His extraordinary religious reforms would shake Egyptian tradition to its foundations and cast a dark and lingering shadow over the entire nation.

Amenhotep IV was crowned King of Egypt in 1352 BC. He married the beautiful Nefertiti and initially continued his father's work by furnishing the temples of Amun with gifts. However, in the second year of his reign there were already indications that the king was moving in an altogether different direction. Temples were erected in the city of Karnak, but on this occasion they were not dedicated to Amun, but instead to the Aten, a deity of the sun. In essence, the Aten was said to be the visible disk of the sun which represented the universal power of Ra, the creator of all life. Whereas Ra was the hidden force behind the sun, the Aten was the visual manifestation of its power, supposedly transcending that of the other gods, and it was on this premise that Amenhotep began to exclusively worship the visible disk. The Theban god Amun was removed from the equation completely and eventually all the other deities were deemed obsolete. This was a shocking and unprecedented move towards monotheism; although Amun-Ra had long been regarded as supreme, the existence of other deities in the Egyptian pantheon had never before been called into question.

The cult of the Aten was central to virtually every decision that Amenhotep made, including changing his name to Akhenaten, meaning 'Servant of the Aten'. Coincidentally, it was also during his reign that the Egyptian king first became known as the *Pharaoh*, a title meaning 'Great House' which previously referred to the royal palace. Such was Akhenaten's vanity that he proclaimed himself and Nefertiti to be the divine children of the Aten, forming a sacred family to be worshipped during the many festivals held throughout his reign. Akhenaten and his family moved to a glittering new capital city, constructed in honour of the Aten and named Akhetaten, meaning 'Horizon of the sun disk'. This was the site where the Amarna letters were later discovered, many of which were composed by Akhenaten himself as he continued the diplomacy practiced by his father. No doubt a relatively passive foreign policy had the advantage of affording him more time to contemplate his radical beliefs.

Whether the Egyptian people supported their self-proclaimed divine leader is doubtful at best; religion aside, he achieved little of substance, as military campaigns were limited to intermittent putting down of rebellions in Palestine and Nubia. There was some limited organised opposition against the regime from conservative elites and the embittered priesthood of Amun in Thebes; however they were unable to prevent matters from worsening as Akhenaten proceeded to outlaw the other gods and remove their names from monuments across the country. It was not long before society came to a standstill: temples were closed and local festivals cancelled as it became disturbingly apparent to the Egyptian people that Akhenaten was enforcing a religious revolution.

The effects were catastrophic. Following the closure of the traditional temples, the priests were unable to collect taxes and the army was ordered to take their place. As governmental powers were centralised, funds were transferred from local temples to the royal palace at Akhetaten, where they were hastily spent on new shrines and statues of the Aten. Opposition voices were silenced as dissenters were tortured or executed. Akhenaten's incessant pursuit of his religious ideals ultimately led to the obliteration of the political and economic fabric of a country that had hitherto been thriving.

It came as a relief to many when the eccentric pharaoh died in 1336 BC, although even after his death the path to liberation from the cult of the Aten was not a straightforward one. After moving to his new capital, Akhenaten had taken another queen, Kiya, whose standing probably improved because she was able to provide him with a male heir. It seems that she later died or fell out of favour with the pharaoh, enabling Nefertiti to resume her role as his favoured wife; however, just before Akhenaten's death, Nefertiti too disappears from the historical record. Some believe she died, ran away, or perhaps moved to Thebes to appease the priests of Amun, but the most popular theory is that she served as co-regent with her husband before ruling alone under the name Neferneferuaten. It is still not known whether this female pharaoh was indeed Nefertiti, but in any case she died soon afterwards. This left Akhenaten's only male heir, the adolescent son of Kiya, to take his place on the throne at the tender age of nine.

The young prince had been named Tutankhaten by his late father, translated as 'the living image of Aten', but finding himself at the forefront of a popular movement to reinstate Amun, he symbolically changed his name to Tutankhamun. Notwithstanding his posthumous infamy, Tutankhamun's reign was actually very short and because he had not yet come of age, it was probably his vizier, Ay, and the commander-in-chief of the army, Horemheb, who directed royal policy between them. Be that as it may, Tutankhamun's explicit association with the redemption of Egypt was reason enough to make him a saviour of the people. Guided by his advisors, he abandoned the city of Akhetaten, encouraged the public to worship Amun-Ra and the other traditional deities and returned the imperial seat of power to Thebes. His decision to consign the cult of the Aten to history and reinstate the other gods won him the lasting affection of the Egyptian people and particularly the Theban priesthood.

Tutankhamun died in 1327 BC, aged just nineteen years old, prematurely ending a period of rule that lasted barely ten years. It appears that his death was caused by gangrene following a fracture of the leg; possibly caused by a fall from his chariot. Despite the brevity of his reign, Tutankhamun was carefully buried alongside his treasure, his body mummified and his face covered with an immaculately crafted golden mask. Because the pharaoh's death was wholly unexpected, his widow, Ankhesenamun, had not produced an heir to the throne and it appears that she later married again to her husband's vizier, Ay, who reigned for just four years before he too passed away. The royal line, dating all the way back to Ahmose, had finally been broken and the kingship consequently passed to Horemheb, who respectfully continued the process of restoring Egyptian society to normality.

The cult of the Aten was a damaging episode and the widely proclaimed heresy of Akhenaten was scorned and condemned by his successors. The cancellation of religious festivals and the prohibition of worship, except of the Aten, had deprived the Egyptian people of their traditions, while the treatment of the priesthood and blatant disrespect shown by the pharaoh to the rest of the celestial hierarchy resulted in both bewilderment and fury. Moreover, Akhenaten's insistence that he was the divine ruler of Egypt led the public to seriously question whether any king of Egypt could legitimately make such a claim again. In order to win back the people's hearts, a new kind of leader would have to emerge; one who would be able to show respect to the traditional gods but also to have the courage to be a warrior and the prowess to contend with a deadly rival that was becoming alarmingly hostile in the Near East.

XVII

As Egypt struggled through its self-induced crisis, the region of Anatolia witnessed the resurgence of the Hittites, led by the courageous King Suppiluliumas, who was crowned in 1344 BC. Charismatic he may have been, but the new king did not entirely act in the spirit of the age. Sharing the same intent as the infamous King Mursilis, two centuries earlier, Suppiluliumas attempted to overcome the Mitannian stronghold of Aleppo and seize control of the northern Euphrates trade route. Although the assault was initially kept at bay by the Mitannians, the Hittite army responded by crossing the river into Syria, besieging the Mitannian capital, Washukkani, and forcing the stunned King Tushratta to flee into the countryside. Showing the more cautious side of his character, Suppiluliumas opted not to repeat the actions of his predecessor by sailing downstream to Babylon, and access to the remainder of the trade route was instead secured by his marriage to a Kassite princess, the daughter of Burnaburiash.

Suppiluliumas had maintained a distant but cordial relationship with Akhenaten; however his feelings towards the Egyptians changed drastically following a diplomatic incident which nearly aligned the two powers permanently, but instead sent them spiralling towards war. After the death of Tutankhamun, the pharaoh's widow, Ankhesenamun, rightly feared that she would have to marry one of her subjects and urgently requested Suppiluliumas to send his son, Prince Zannanza, to join her in marriage and become the next pharaoh. The Hittite king obliged and the prince began the long journey to Egypt, only to be murdered on route, allegedly at the command of the vizier, Ay, who went on to marry the queen and become the next pharaoh himself. Suppiluliumas was furious and after an angry exchange of letters he retaliated by marching south into Egyptian territory, where he promptly captured the city of Qadesh.

The New Kingdom of Hatti was administered in the same rigorous manner as the Old Kingdom, with local governors and puppet rulers stationed in each of its foreign territories and enforcing the payment of taxes on a regular basis. The army consisted of some thirty thousand Hittite soldiers, supplemented by a significant number of mercenaries from the vassal states and divided into infantry and charioteers. Their success served to popularise the myth that in c.1500 BC the Hittites had discovered how to make iron and used it to develop superior weapons to overpower their bronze-wielding neighbours. However although it is true that the process of smelting iron was developed in Anatolia at around this time, there is actually no evidence that the Hittites held a monopoly of iron and in fact the mass production of iron weapons does not appear to have taken place until after 1200 BC. Instead it is more likely that the Hittite achievements were aided by firm and decisive leadership and the uncharacteristically passive approach of the other great powers at the time.

The inspirational Suppiluliumas died prematurely of illness in 1322 BC and the Hittite throne passed to his eldest son, Mursilis II. With the tension mounting between the Hittites and Egyptians, Mursilis refrained from expansionist policies and instead focused on cementing Hatti's dominant position in Anatolia. A successful campaign in the west enforced a pro-Hittite ruler upon the Arzawa lands, while smaller neighbouring kingdoms were converted into vassal states. The next king, Muwatallis, faced an immediate crisis when Hattusas was attacked once again by the Gasga tribes from the north, but the city's defences held firm. As a precautionary measure, the capital was moved to the southern city of Karaman as the Hittites sought to avoid a repeat of the local Anatolian uprisings which had previously led to the collapse of the Old Kingdom. This time they had greater forces to contend with.

XVIII

Back in the Nile Valley, Horemheb had not fathered any children and therefore nominated another military man, Pramessu, as the heir to the throne. Pramessu came to power in 1295 BC and promptly changed his name to Ramesses, meaning 'Ra bore him'. Ramesses was already old at the time of his succession and died just a year later, leaving his son, Seti, to take up the mantle of restoring faith to the Egyptian monarchy. The new pharaoh achieved this by outwardly expressing his admiration for the great leaders of the past, assisted by the compilation of a definitive list of kings. Conspicuously the kings of the Amarna period were omitted and the legitimate rule of Egypt was said to have passed directly from Amenhotep III to Horemheb. Seti dedicated much of his reign to the foundation and restoration of traditional temples and monuments, many of which were completed by Nubian slaves.

The pharaoh also took steps to improve Egypt's foreign interests. Successful campaigns were waged against the Libyans and rebellious city-states in the Levant and the Egyptian army eventually made its way to Qadesh; the stronghold which had become established as the main frontier between Egypt and Hatti. The Hittites were taken aback by the unexpected Egyptian advance and Muwattalis warily bided his time by making peace with Seti. The period of calm that followed gave both sides time to prepare for an almighty clash which at this stage must have seemed inevitable.

In 1279 BC, the death of Seti enabled the succession of one of Egypt's greatest and most formidable leaders: the illustrious Ramesses II. The quintessential warrior-king, Ramesses was destined to become a hero in the eyes of the Egyptian people. The first clue to his ambitions was when he moved the capital from

Thebes to the city of Piramesse; a more strategic location in the delta as it lay closer to the enemy. Piramesse was essentially an expansion of the old Hyksos capital, Avaris; a cosmopolitan centre with an enduring Asiatic influence. It was an interesting choice which emphasised the pharaoh's recognition that Egypt was intrinsically tied to the Near East. Indeed, the relocation to the delta proved to be of immediate importance as Ramesses was forced to defend the Nile from pirates in only his second year in power. Following the Egyptian naval victory, the pirates were drafted into the army, just in time for the greater battle which lay ahead.

Three years later, in 1274 BC, Ramesses led his troops into the Levant and purposefully marched towards Qadesh and the Hittite border. Lying in wait were fifty thousand Hittite soldiers, including mercenaries and slaves from their vassal territories. Ramesses had been led to believe that Muwatallis had shied away from battle, but in fact the Hittite King was patiently waiting with his men on the northern fringes of Qadesh. In a tactical masterstroke, Muwatallis allowed the first Egyptian division to enter the city walls before launching a fearsome attack on the second division which was left hugely outnumbered and became easy prey for the Hittite charioteers. The Hittites then turned on the first division, which was stranded in the city, and prepared to strike a devastating blow.

It was at this moment that Ramesses claims to have cried out to Amun for help, and his request was seemingly granted as another wave of Egyptian soldiers appeared from out of nowhere and swept into the Hittite infantrymen from behind, enabling the beleaguered pharaoh to escape from the clutches of disaster. Gradually more Egyptian divisions entered the fray and suddenly it was the Hittites who were surrounded, but they too defended themselves valiantly and the battle soon descended into a stalemate. As the bloodshed engulfed both sides, Muwattalis offered to make peace. Ramesses obdurately rejected this out of hand, but did agree to a truce.

Ultimately neither side had done enough to defeat the other and the battle ended in a draw, but this did not prevent the pharaoh from marching exultantly back to the delta, claiming an emphatic victory. In an audacious show of propaganda, Ramesses hailed the moment when Amun answered his prayers and came to his aid, inspiring him to singlehandedly turn the battle on its head and force the Hittites to beg for peace. His account of the conflict was etched onto the walls of his temples and the Egyptian people duly praised their hero for his courageous and splendid success. Of course the reality was a completely different story; although the Egyptians had not been defeated, strategically the Hittites had won a great victory as they not only managed to repel the Egyptian advance and achieve their aim of maintaining control of Syria, but once the Egyptian army returned home, Muwattalis wasted no time before seizing several city-states south of Qadesh.

As it transpired, the Hittite occupation was short-lived. After a brief interlude, during which Egypt concentrated on defending its western border from hostile Libyan nomads, Ramesses led his revitalised army back to the Levant. One by one the city-states swore their allegiance to the pharaoh and Qadesh was recaptured without opposition from the Hittites, whose attention had been diverted by the looming threat of Assyria. Finally, in 1258 BC, sixteen years after they had fought in battle, the great powers of Egypt and Hatti acknowledged their conflict had become futile and agreed to sign a peace treaty; the first of its kind in history. Much emphasis was given to a defensive alliance, presumably aimed at the Assyrians.

By the time of his death in 1213 BC, Ramesses had already become a legend among his people. He reigned for an incredible sixty seven years and although he failed to defeat the Hittites, the Egyptian Empire was strengthened and emboldened from Syria to Nubia. More than just a warlord, the pharaoh's sentimental side was epitomised by a genuine love for his first wife, Nefertari, for whom he dedicated temples and composed verses of romantic poetry, to be inscribed upon the walls of her burial chamber. Needless to say, their relationship was not exclusive and Ramesses had a further seven wives, including four of his own daughters, while he fathered over a hundred children. Conceited and egotistical he may have been, but Ramesses had a charismatic presence to match any of his predecessors, breathing life into Egypt and giving his people a renewed sense of pride. At the same time, the confrontation with the Hittites had made them deeply aware of the dangers that lurked beyond Egypt's borders, simmering far away on the blood-stained battlefields of the Near East.

XIX

The land of Assyria was one of the world's oldest civilizations, coexisting with the ancient kingdom of Sumer and predating the arrival of the Indo-Europeans. The settlement of Assur was founded in the Third Millennium BC on the western bank of the Tigris and it quickly rose to become an influential city-state, presiding over trading colonies as far as Anatolia. The supreme god of Assyria was also called Assur and was worshipped as the patron of the city and the surrounding land. Everything the Assyrians strove for was committed in the name of Assur, which only served to intensify the shame they felt at being subjected to foreign rule. Indeed, as resentment towards their oppressors increased, so the desire for vengeance grew stronger by the year.

Under the brave leadership of Assur-uballit in the Fourteenth Century BC, Assyria began to shake off its Mitannian shackles and expanded into the eastern plains of the Tigris. The Assyrian drive towards independence was accelerated by an internal dispute in Mitanni following King Tushratta's humiliating defeat to the Hittites, whereafter the unpopular king was murdered as part of a conspiracy led by his brother, Artatama. Tushratta's son and legitimate heir, Mattiwaza, fled to Hatti and returned to defeat Artatama, largely as a result of support from the Hittite army. The conflict led to the partitioning of Mitannian territory by the Hittites in the west and the Assyrians in the east, leaving Mattiwaza to preside over a small vassal territory, subservient to the Hittite king. As the Hittites became preoccupied with confronting Egypt, Assyria took advantage by making further territorial gains and eradicating the last remnants of the Mitannian state.

Having lost their buffer, the Hittites faced a powerful Assyrian adversary on their eastern border and feared the loss of the Euphrates trade route. The situation in Hatti was worsened by a domestic quarrel following the death of Muwattalis, whose illegitimate son, Urhi-Teshub, was eventually usurped by his uncle, Hattusilis III, in 1267 BC. Preoccupied by instability at home and anticipating an Assyrian attack, Hattusilis signed the aforementioned treaty with Egypt and concluded a further defensive alliance with Babylonia. Yet the Assyrian advance was relentless, particularly during the reign of King Shalmaneser, who marched as far as Carchemish on the western bank of the Euphrates. By the time Hattusilis was succeeded by Tudhaliyas IV in 1237 BC, Shalmaneser had seized Hatti's copper mines, prompting the Hittites to invade Cyprus to source alternative supplies. The Hittite army managed to stall the Assyrian advance at Carchemish and the intended invasion was curtailed, but this did not disguise the mounting problems facing Hatti. Most worrying of all was a series of failed harvests which meant that grain had to be imported from Egypt. Once a great power, the kingdom of Hatti was now in terminal decline.

Assyrian ambitions were also evident in southern Mesopotamia. Throughout the Kassite period, the rivalry between Babylonia and Assyria was characterised by border skirmishes which intensified as the latter grew in strength. This increasingly volatile relationship was occasionally tempered by diplomatic measures, but the situation was enflamed in 1225 BC when the Assyrian King, Tukulti-Ninurta, sacked Babylon and carried the Kassite king and the holy statue of Marduk back to Assur. The Babylonians were beside themselves with anger and distress, but despite a succession of puppet rulers installed by the Assyrians, there was to be no permanent suppression of Babylon. Instead, the locals rebelled again and reinstated the displaced Kassite dynasty. Ironically, the main consequence of the Assyrian invasion was the spread of Babylonian culture as numerous tablets and works of art were transported to Assur for the perusal of Assyrian nobles and scholars.

As the world prepared to enter the Twelfth Century BC, the kingdoms of the Near East reflected upon a sequence of events that had ruptured the balance of power and witnessed the obliteration of Mitanni, the severe weakening of Hatti and Babylon and the steady rise of Assyria. It might have been expected that an Assyrian Empire would materialise and eventually come into conflict with Egypt, but in 1207 BC Tukulti-Ninurta was assassinated in a rebellion led by his own sons and Assyria descended into internal strife, abandoning its expansionist plans in the process. Instead, an unforeseen wave of change was about to engulf the whole Near East and eastern Mediterranean, with a greater impact than anything since the arrival of the Indo-Europeans. These were dangerous yet fascinating times.

XX

While the great powers of the Near East competed for pre-eminence, Mycenaean Greece continued to function primarily as a trading outlet, exporting desirable goods from the Aegean, coastal Anatolia and the barbaric lands of Europe. Yet although the Mycenaeans operated on the periphery of the civilized world, migratory movements and conflicts in the Aegean were to have an immediate and lasting effect on the entire region. This period of turmoil was marked by a legendary event that probably took place in the early Twelfth Century BC, known to posterity as the Trojan War.

The settlement of Troy was founded on the western coast of Anatolia towards the end of the Fourth Millennium BC, at around the beginning of the Bronze Age. Anatolia imported many ideas and customs from early civilized societies in Mesopotamia, including the notion of a city-state, and before long Troy rose to become an important urban centre within a wider region that later became known as the Troad. Like countless other settlements in the ancient world, Troy was destroyed and reconstructed on several occasions, but by the second half of the Second Millennium BC it had developed into a magnificent and wealthy city, overlooking fertile plains and protected by imposing city walls.

This was the setting of *The Iliad*, an epic poem believed to have been written in the Eighth Century BC by the Greek poet, Homer. *The Iliad* depicts the legend of the Trojan War and later inspired a series of classical poems and plays on the same theme. Collectively, they tell the story of Helen, the beautiful wife of King Menelaus of Sparta, who was seduced by Paris, a Trojan Prince, and persuaded to elope with him to Troy. Menelaus was outraged at losing his beloved Helen and called upon the assistance of his brother, Agamemnon, to bring her back. As King of Mycenae, Agamemnon held the most powerful position in Mycenaean Greece. He duly assembled an army of soldiers from the many Greek kingdoms and together they sailed across the Aegean Sea in over a thousand ships. The Greeks, known to Homer as the Achaeans, set up camp on the Anatolian coast, upon the fringes of an open plain which separated them from King Priam's fortified city of Troy.

For ten years, the Achaeans and Trojans fought in battles influenced by the will of Zeus and his fellow immortals upon Mount Olympus. Eventually the Achaeans gained the upper hand when their greatest warrior, Achilles, defeated Priam's strongest son, Hector. Yet despite their vast numbers, the Achaeans were unable to penetrate the unassailable city walls, until the master tactician Odysseus had a brilliant idea. He persuaded his fellow soldiers to build a giant wooden horse, large enough for several men to hide inside. The rest of the army then sailed away from the shore so they appeared to have abandoned their camp, leaving the wooden horse to stand alone on the beach. The Trojans, believing the horse to be a gift, carried it back to Troy and returned to Priam's palace. As Trojan soldiers and citizens alike celebrated what they thought was a resounding victory, the Achaeans crept out of the horse and lit fires to signal to their fleet that they were inside the city. The gates were opened and thousands of Achaeans poured into Troy, annihilating the unsuspecting Trojans and burning the city to the ground.

For centuries there have been arguments for and against the historical reality of the Trojan War and historians have long since attempted to unravel the truth behind the legend. The Trojans were certainly less conspicuous than the great powers of their time, but it is now commonly believed they were among the Luwian peoples; the first of the Indo-European groups to arrive in Anatolia, who settled on the western shores and became a frequent source of irritation to the Hittites. The Luwians established several small kingdoms, together known as the Arzawa lands, and one of these kingdoms, the north-western territory of *Wilusa*, appears to have been the Hittite name for Troy.

Relations between Troy and Mycenaean Greece were peaceful for long periods and, despite their close proximity to the Hittite realm, the Trojans appear to have traded almost exclusively with their Aegean neighbours. The Mycenaeans were evidently unfazed by the presence of the Hittites and even founded a trading colony at Miletus, just as the Minoans had done before them. The foundation of a colony in Anatolia is unlikely to have gone unnoticed in Hatti, and although there is still much debate on the subject, it appears the Hittites were aware of Mycenaean Greece and referred to it as *Ahhiyawa*. This state was described as a threat in Hittite records, following its repeated attempts to invoke uprisings in the Arzawa lands, indicating the Greeks did indeed have a military presence in western Anatolia around the time of the Trojan War.

There is no doubt that Hatti possessed superior strength to both the Trojans and Mycenaean Greeks and it is therefore surprising that Homer does not make a single reference to the Hittites in *The Iliad*. This may be explained by the possibility that, by the time of the Trojan War, the Hittite Empire had been completely dismantled and the Arzawa lands had regained their independence. Without the risk of facing the Hittite army, the Mycenaeans could have engaged in direct conflict with Troy, possibly to secure the maritime passage to the Black Sea, or simply to plunder an affluent city. It must be said that the possibility of the Greeks suddenly turning against their key trading partner is curious and suggests that some kind of feud may have been behind it. It was not unknown for a king to go to war for family reasons, such as when King Suppiluliumas of the Hittites avenged the Egyptians for murdering his son, so it is not inconceivable that a royal love triangle could have had such an impact. Although the true nature of the war may never be revealed, it is beyond doubt that the Trojans were defeated by someone;

archaeological evidence confirms that Troy was destroyed by warfare in the early Twelfth Century BC.

Over the years, Greek bards retold the story, gradually elevating it to an epic by emphasising the role of the gods and the endeavours of the courageous Achaean and Trojan warriors. Of course, in all probability they exaggerated certain factors, such as the length of the war, the number of ships that sailed across the Aegean, and possibly the role of a royal love affair in sparking the conflict. Indeed, it must be remembered that the Trojan War has only gained infamy because of the great literary works that have survived to tell the tale. The historical evidence suggests it was a relatively insignificant local struggle, only made possible by the waning of the Hittite Empire. As enterprising as the Mycenaeans had become, they were still vastly inferior to the greatest powers of the ancient world and remained susceptible to any concentrated attack from elsewhere. This vulnerability became all too apparent in the years that followed the conquest of Troy.

XXI

In *The Odyssey*, Homer describes the myriad of troubles encountered by the Achaean warriors as they returned home from Troy, focusing on the afflictions of the heroic Odysseus of Ithica. He also refers to disorder in the Greek cities, not least in Mycenae where King Agamemnon was murdered by his wife Clytemnestra and her lover, Aegisthus, before they in turn were killed in vengeance by Agamemnon's son, Orestes. These legendary events were characteristic of the chaos and growing social unrest within Mycenaean society in the Twelfth Century BC, culminating in the tragic decline of an iconic civilization. As unity among the various kingdoms disintegrated, the major cities became isolated and vulnerable, and settlements such as Mycenae and Pylos were ravaged by a succession of fires that swept across the country. Only Athens escaped the devastation. The most convincing explanation for these events is that the Mycenaean cities had fallen to invaders, although it is by no means certain where they came from or why they decided to invade.

Greek mythology attests that the invaders were descendants of the legendary hero Heracles, the son of Zeus and a mortal woman named Alcmene. Zeus intended that Heracles would rule the Peloponnese, but the supreme god's adultery incurred the wrath of his immortal wife, Hera, who ensured that King Eurystheus of Tiryns would rule instead. Hera bore a lasting grudge against Heracles and persistently intervened in his life to appease her anger. She briefly drove him to madness, causing him to murder three of his own children, and entrusted Eurystheus to punish him for the crime. The punishment was the twelve labours: a sequence of perilous challenges that required him to overcome terrifying beasts such as a nine-headed serpent and man-eating horses. Heracles successfully completed the labours, but when he finally passed away, his family was banished to the backwater of Thessaly in northern Greece. Dismayed at their exile, his descendants, the Heracleidae, vowed to one day return to the Peloponnese to reclaim their right to rule.

The classical Greeks identified the return of the Heracleidae with the invasion of the Dorians; a tribe who spoke a different dialect of Greek to the established Achaeans. Although the nature and timing of a Dorian invasion is disputed, there is little doubt they arrived in Greece much later than the Achaeans and it is certainly conceivable that their arrival brought about the death knell of Mycenaean civilization. The Dorians appear to have been driven southwards by tribal movements in the Balkans and eventually settled in the Peloponnese, probably by violent means, forcing many of the Achaean inhabitants to abandon their homes and flee to the east. Those who remained were enslaved and in due course became the helots of Sparta and the other Dorian cities.

The native Achaeans consisted of two distinct tribes, known as Ionians and Aeolians. Both groups had scattered across Greece by the time the Dorians arrived, but the Ionians were particularly identifiable with Attica and its principal city, Athens, while the Aeolians were mainly associated with Thessaly and Boeotia. Following the Dorian invasions, many Ionians and Aeolians were compelled to resettle in the Aegean islands and coastal regions of western Anatolia which thereafter became known as Ionia and Aeolis. The Dorians also spread across the Aegean and founded cities in Crete and an area of Anatolia to the south of Ionia. These settlements would eventually form part of a glorious Hellenic civilization, encompassing the entire Aegean. However centuries would pass before this transpired. The immediate situation was that Mycenaean society had disappeared and Greece had descended into the dark ages.

Meanwhile, the deteriorating kingdom of Hatti was finally put out of its misery by another group of migrants from the north. The invaders were the Phrygians and they slowly made their way from Thrace to Anatolia, probably during the same period as the Dorian invasions. The old Hittite capital, Hattussas, was captured, if it had not already been vacated, and this time there would be no Hittite resurgence. The exiled royal family found temporary solace in Carchemish and continued to claim descent from the kings of yesteryear, but in these rapidly changing times, the kingdom of Hatti was soon to become a distant memory. The descendants of the Hittites formed several small kingdoms with limited influence in the Near East, although one of these states, Lydia, would eventually command its own empire.

The invasions in Greece and Anatolia thrust many people from their homes, including the inhabitants of the Aegean islands and the coastal Arzawa lands. To try and ensure their survival, these embittered refugees hastily launched a coordinated attempt to seize foreign territory for themselves. Known to the Egyptians as the 'Sea Peoples', they were armed with iron weapons and wreaked havoc along the Levantine coast, overcoming Cyprus and the region of Cilicia in southern Anatolia. They continued to march southwards through Syria and Palestine, where arguably the most famous group of Sea Peoples, the Philistines, eventually formed their own state. Finally, the army of refugees arrived at the Egyptian border, where they made an audacious attempt to invade the land of the pharaohs.

Egypt had been left in a stable position by the great Ramesses II, but during the reign of his son and immediate successor, Merneptah, the Sea Peoples initiated their first attack on the delta. The invaders allied with tribes from Libya, amounting to a sizeable force. They took with them their wives, children and possessions, clearly intent on settling in the land they sought to conquer. Although the onslaught took the Egyptians by surprise, Merneptah's army responded purposefully and drove the Sea Peoples away, killing thousands in the process. This gave Egypt a brief period of respite; however in 1177 BC, the Sea Peoples returned with reinforcements and instigated a second assault. They approached on two fronts, over land and sea, but on this occasion the Egyptians, now led by Ramesses III, were fully prepared and met the invaders with an effective defence force in both Palestine and the delta. The land attack was repelled almost immediately, although the Egyptian fleet had to engage in a fierce battle in the Nile before emerging victorious. Defeated for a second time, the Sea Peoples finally discarded their ambitions in Egypt, leaving Ramesses to bask in glory.

Unfortunately for the pharaoh, this proved to be the swan song of Egyptian power. The country was rocked by an assassination conspiracy against him, masterminded by his second wife, Queen Tiye, who wanted her son, Pentaweret, to succeed to the throne. The plan was to murder the pharaoh during the annual festival at Thebes in a stratagem which appears to have been heavily dependent on witchcraft practised by women in the royal harem. In the end the plot failed and resulted in seventeen executions and seven suicides, including Pentaweret himself, but the episode also created a lingering atmosphere of mistrust within the royal palace. Under Ramesses' successors, Egypt fell swiftly into decline. The ill-conceived policy of transferring land to the priesthood backfired as the state began to lose control of the economy, resulting in rising grain prices and labour strikes. Territorial losses in Palestine and Nubia were compounded by an influx of Libyan nomads, while a lack of funds prevented the construction of new temples and statues which may have gone some way towards appeasing the disillusioned public. Another eight successive kings bore the name 'Ramesses', but this was all they shared with the famous statesman they sought to emulate.

From the Eleventh Century BC, the extent of Egypt's demise is truly heart-rending. Famine and civil war ravaged the country and there were a series of tomb robberies as Libyan bandits stole the riches that had been bestowed upon the dead. Worse was to come: following a military coup led by General Piankh, the removal of treasure from the Valley of the Kings became official state policy and even the mummified pharaohs were unwrapped to salvage the precious gifts that had been placed upon their bodies. Only the carefully concealed tomb of Tutankhamun was left unspoiled. In the coming years, centralised government evaporated completely and the Egyptian people were humiliatingly subjected to periods of Libyan and Nubian rule. In a country preoccupied by the rites of death, the golden era of Egyptian civilization had finally been laid to rest.

The fortunes of the Babylonians were not much better. Having been invaded by Assyria at the end of the Thirteenth Century BC and subjected to a painful period of subordination to Assur, they next found themselves at the mercy of the Elamites; the old enemy who had been kept relatively quiet since their infamous defeat at the hands of Hammurabi. The final act of the long Kassite dynasty came in 1155 BC when the Elamite king, Shutruk-Nahhunte, led his army into Babylon, plundered the city, and returned to Susa with as many treasures as he could lay his hands on, including, of course, the famous statue of Marduk. Although the collapse of Kassite rule was unrelated to the invasions in Greece and Anatolia or the migrations of the Sea Peoples, Mesopotamia would have been left vulnerable by the loss of trading contacts in the west and it is therefore not surprising that this region too fell to invaders.

By the time the Elamite army withdrew, Babylonia had splintered into regional kingdoms. One of these, founded in the old Sumerian city of Isin, emerged as the self-appointed leader of the Babylonians and under the rule of King Nebuchadnezzar there was a brief, but celebrated renaissance. In 1120 BC, taking advantage of domestic problems inside Elam, Nebuchadnezzar marched into Susa, reclaimed the statue of Marduk and with it, the faith and pride of his people. The king's name was to be fondly remembered by future generations for his spirited vengeance on the detested Elamites. Unfortunately, whilst the dignity of Babylonia had been preserved, Nebuchadnezzar's successors were unable to resurrect the peaceful prosperity of the Kassite era, and without the protection of a strong centralised state, many people abandoned the cities for a nomadic lifestyle in the countryside. The same scenario took place in Elam, whose quick reversal of fortunes had propelled the kingdom back into obscurity. Accordingly, southern Mesopotamia followed her western neighbours into the dark ages. The political and cultural framework of the Near East would soon bare a very different complexion.

XXII

In the Eleventh and Tenth Centuries BC, the Near East fragmented into small kingdoms, surrounded by rural communities and nomadic tribes. One of the main developments in this period was the gradual replacement of bronze with iron, leading to the inception of an Iron Age. Iron had actually been produced throughout much of the Bronze Age, but following important advances in the smelting process, metallurgists at the end of the Second Millennium BC began to add specific amounts of carbon to produce steel; a much stronger metal than bronze. The recent upheavals in the Near East had resulted in the closure of many trade routes, making it increasingly difficult to source supplies of copper and tin, so the transition was timely. The power of iron weaponry was first demonstrated on a major scale by the Sea Peoples and it soon became essential for a warrior to be clad and armed with iron.

Another consequence of the Twelfth Century invasions was the settlement and expansion of migratory tribes in regions that had previously been controlled by the great empires. The most prominent were the Arameans; a roving tribe of Semitic pastoralists from the Syrian Desert who began to exploit land that had once been occupied by the Hittites. In the absence of an imperial power to thwart their progress, the Arameans ventured down the Euphrates, forming clusters of settlements that bordered Assyria and Babylonia. Despite their barbaric culture, they began to dominate Mesopotamia and consequently the Aramaic language became widespread, replacing Akkadian as the *lingua franca* of the Near East.

It was not just the Arameans who were making a name for themselves. Also emerging from the desert, this time in Arabia, were the Arabs; another group of Semitic people. The domestication of the camel enabled the Arabs to reach the fringes of Mesopotamia and the Levant, where they traded in exotic goods such as frankincense and myrrh. Further north, in central Anatolia, the vacuum left by the collapse of the Hittite Empire was filled by a number of relatively weak states which became known as the Neo-Hittite kingdoms. Meanwhile, beyond the Tigris in the east, a new faction of Indo-European migrants arrived from the shores of the Caspian Sea. They consisted of autonomous tribes known as the Medes and Persians, and they soon began to occupy large swathes of territory to the east of the Zagros Mountains. For the time being they did not interfere in Mesopotamian affairs, but their impact in later centuries was to be immense.

On the subject of inconspicuous groups whose influence was to grow to unimaginable levels, it was also during this period that an earlier group of Semitic migrants settled in a region of the Levant that would later be known as Israel. Biblical tradition attests that a wandering tribe called the Hebrews originally followed their leader, Abraham, from Ur to the Levantine region of Canaan in c.1850 BC. Abraham was succeeded by his son, Isaac, and then by his grandson, Jacob (the Three Patriarchs) but during the lifetime of the latter, the onset of famine and increasing competition for resources with the native Canaanites compelled the Hebrews to abandon the area and resettle in the Nile delta. According to the Bible, Jacob was renamed 'Israel' by an angel and his descendants thereafter became known as the Israelites, divided into twelve tribes which were each named after one of his sons.

Over six hundred years later, probably during the reign of Ramesses II, the Israelites were forced to flee the pharaoh's oppressive regime in Egypt and were led eastwards through the Sinai Desert by their inspirational leader, Moses. They returned to Canaan and forcefully established their own towns and villages under Moses' successor, Joshua, before engaging in a series of wars with the Philistines; one of the Sea Peoples who had settled in the region following their failed assault on Egypt. This prompted the twelve tribes to unite and form a monarchical state which was to be known as the Kingdom of Israel. Shortly after 1000 BC, King David's Israelites overcame the Philistines and Canaanites and designated the small town of Jerusalem as their capital city. Under David's successor, the wise and exceptionally wealthy King Solomon, a holy temple was built in Jerusalem in commemoration.

The story of the Hebrews would have been of little significance to communities outside Canaan and would surely have been reduced to a footnote in history, had it not been for their extraordinary religious innovations which vastly transcended their military achievements. Essentially they believed in just one god, whom they called Yahweh. During the exodus from Egypt, Yahweh was said to have agreed a covenant with the children of Israel, promising them a safe return to Canaan in exchange for obedience to his laws, known as *The Ten Commandments*. He was also said to have revealed the first five books of the Bible (the *Torah*) to Moses, which included the story of the creation of the world and the lives of the Patriarchs, followed by an exposition of fundamental requirements of faith, including circumcision and *kosher* dietary restrictions. The Torah remains the most sacred part of the Hebrew Bible.

The ancient world had dabbled in monotheism before, notably during the reign of Akhenaten in Egypt and to an extent through the pre-eminence of favoured deities, such as Marduk in Babylon and Assur in Assyria, but never before had a society completely abandoned polytheistic traditions and replaced them with a solitary, all-powerful god. The first united Kingdom of Israel lasted less than a hundred years before it split into two kingdoms, Israel and Judah, but its legacy was unsurpassable; not only did the Hebrew religion, Judaism, eventually spread across the world, but its monotheistic doctrine inspired the religions of Christianity and Islam, and all the political and social implications that came with them.

XXIII

Arguably the most enterprising people of the new Millennium were a group of seafarers whose home was to the north of Canaan, on the eastern shores of the Mediterranean. The origin of the Phoenicians is uncertain, but they appear to have arrived as early as the Fourteenth Century BC, possibly from near the Gulf. City-states were established in Phoenicia, the most distinguished of which were Tyre, Sidon and Byblos, and each was ruled by an independent monarch, in a similar fashion to Mycenaean Greece. The location of the various city-states, with easy access to Egypt, the Aegean and Mesopotamia, was ideal for establishing a trading network, and by the Twelfth Century BC the Phoenicians were renowned as the leading merchants in the ancient world. Although Sidon was besieged by the Philistines during the invasion of the Sea Peoples, the Phoenicians managed to ride out the storm and rose to become one of the defining groups of the early Iron Age.

The Phoenicians learned the methods of the Mycenaeans and their own trading empire was enhanced by the excellent reputation of their craftsmanship in a variety of fields, including textiles, glassmaking, carpentry and metallurgy. The emphasis was on style and elegance and Phoenician goods soon became popular throughout the Mediterranean and Near East. Specialities included a unique purple dye, made in Tyre, and luxury fabrics woven from silk. Interestingly though, the most significant export was not a material substance, but an idea; it was the Phoenicians who developed the classical alphabet that was adopted and circulated far and wide, by the Greeks in Europe and the Arameans in Asia.

As the Phoenicians began to dominate Mediterranean trade, they took advantage of the situation by founding trading colonies in strategic locations such as Egypt, Cyprus, and Sicily. The merchants were extremely resourceful and all the raw materials and finished goods from these locations were efficiently loaded onto their ships and transported to wherever there was sufficient demand. Nothing was off limits and the Phoenicians actively encouraged the slave trade, which routinely included prisoners of war and young children who had been exchanged for desirable goods. As profits soared, the Phoenician sailors became more adventurous and were particularly enticed by the coastline of northern Africa which had provisions of exotic goods such as ebony, ivory, and a variety of animal skins and horns. They also explored the western Mediterranean, where they established colonies in southern Spain and proceeded to source valuable supplies of silver.

For centuries, the civilized societies of the Mediterranean and Near East believed that the narrow strait of Gibraltar, separating the Iberian Peninsula from Africa, was the gateway to the edge of the world, where the sun descended into the underworld and journeyed beneath the earth before resurfacing in the east the following morning. Yet despite the widely held belief that they were sailing to their deaths, the Phoenicians daringly navigated their ships through the strait into the imposing vastness of the Atlantic Ocean. Having survived this ordeal, they continued northwards along the western coast of Gaul to Cornwall and the Scilly Isles, where they discovered large quantities of tin. Although the Phoenicians opted not to settle in Britain, the sailors returned home with wonderful stories about the native people who grew long beards and wore black cloaks as they moved around with their cattle. According to the classical Greek historian, Herodotus, the Phoenicians later went on to complete the circumnavigation of Africa; a truly remarkable feat for the time if his sources were correct.

The Phoenician outlook was always to the seas rather than inland and it is therefore not surprising that one of the colonies, the city of Carthage, would eventually become more powerful than the cities in Phoenicia itself. There may be some truth in the mythical story of its foundation, centred on the joint heirs to the Tyrian throne, Elissa and Pygmalion. After their father's death, Elissa married her uncle, Acerbas, who served as High Priest and possessed substantial wealth. Following a revolution in Tyre, Pygmalion became the sole monarch, but he also had ambitions to claim Acerbas' gold for himself and took it upon himself to murder his brother-in-law in the holy temple. Elissa was distraught at the death of her husband and was filled with hatred for Pygmalion. She had been ordered to send her husband's treasure to the royal palace, but instead she tricked Pygmalion's men by throwing bags full of sand into the sea, while keeping the gold hidden in her own possession. Elissa then set sail with her followers to northern Africa and founded the settlement of Carthage, never again returning to Tyre. Ironically, it was the survival of Carthage which preserved the independence of the Phoenicians; for the original cities of Phoenicia were soon to be consumed by a new empire in the Near East.

XXIV

The political landscape at the end of the Tenth Century BC was vastly different to that which prevailed before the dark ages, and certainly no state could claim to dominate the rest. There were Phoenicians, Philistines and Israelites in the west, bands of wandering Arabs in the south, isolated tribes of Medes and Persians beyond the Zagros Mountains in the east, fledgling Neo-Hittite kingdoms in the north and numerous independent Aramean settlements, stretching across the whole of Mesopotamia from the Syrian Desert to Babylonia. Outside the Near East, the Greek world was still rebuilding, while the once proud civilization of Egypt had been reduced to a shadow of its former self. The stage was set for a new power to emerge and when it came there would be no state with the strength or resources to resist it.

The land of Assyria, centred on the holy city of Assur on the western bank of the Tigris, came very close to being overrun by Arameans during the early dark ages, and may not have survived but for the courage of Tiglath-Pileser, an energetic monarch who staunchly defended Assyria's borders and then pursued the invaders across the Euphrates. As his army marched into enemy territory, Tiglath-Pileser became the first Assyrian king to receive tribute from city-states in the Levant, while he also captured Babylon after a successful campaign in southern Mesopotamia. After the king's death in 1076 BC, the Arameans closed in around Assyria's borders again and the state fell into decline, but Tiglath-Pileser had at least shown his people a fleeting glimpse of what it was like to rule an empire.

The first king to follow his example was King Adad-nirari II, who came to the throne in 911 BC and forced the Arameans to abandon their settlements in the Assyrian heartland for a second time. This gave the Assyrians some breathing space and enabled them to fortify Assur and increase their military readiness. Their intentions were no longer just about survival, but on winning the spoils of war. The justification was religious, with the campaigns fought as crusades to punish all those who did not believe in the pre-eminent god, Assur. While there is no doubt that Assyrian policy was influenced by religious ideals, there is also an overriding sense of shameless imperialism, driven by the greed of its despotic kings. As the financial rewards became apparent, the predisposition for war became enshrined in the mindset of every Assyrian king, often at the expense of basic human benevolence.

In the early Ninth Century BC, Adad-nirari's grandson, King Assurnasirpal II, set a benchmark for Assyrian brutality and gained a notorious reputation for uncompromising warfare and punishment. He had a penchant for sadism and was known for impaling, decapitating and flaying his enemies before displaying their bodies in public. He particularly liked to build a pyramid of human heads to mark each conquest. There were a great many victims; during his reign the Assyrian army caused havoc across the Near East, demanding tribute from Babylon, Carchemish and the Aramean territories. Arguably the cruellest king ever to rule in the Near East, Assurnasirpal created a climate of fear among Assyria's adversaries that his successors would exploit to the full. Of course, back home it was a different story; the king dedicated his victories to the god Assur and furnished the land with exotic flowers, trees and animals. He also built a new royal city named Kalhu (later known as Nimrud) which was founded on the eastern side of the Tigris and was therefore protected against Aramean raids.

Assurnasirpal's successor, Shalmaneser III, was another warrior king whose thirst for battle kept him away from the royal palace in Kalhu for most of his reign, but with considerably less success. In

853 BC a large coalition army, including forces from Damascus, Israel, Byblos and Egypt, met the Assyrians at the site of Qarqar, on the banks of the River Orontes. Shalmaneser claimed victory after the encounter, but fought no further campaigns in Syria for several years, indicating that the defensive alliance had at least wounded the Assyrian army. When the coalition fell apart in 841 BC, the Assyrians marched back into the region and defeated the Israelites, but Damascus stood firm and showed that the men from Assur were not the invincible force that many believed them to be. Ultimately Shalmanaser's reign was tainted with missed opportunities and failure. Although control of northern Mesopotamia was retained, his attempts to extend Assyrian hegemony into new regions were thwarted by the Armenians, Medes and Persians, and had the undesirable effect of encouraging these tribes to build up their military capabilities. Elsewhere, in the Aramean and Neo-Hittite kingdoms, the main consequence of Assyrian aggression was the formation of further defensive alliances to resist the imperialist foe.

As Shalmaneser grew old, his commander-in-chief, Dayyan-Assur, began to take control of the army in his place; a controversial decision which enraged the crown prince, Assurdaninpal. The embittered heir won sympathy from many disaffected nobles who also felt aggrieved at losing influence to military commanders, and together they plotted to overthrow the ageing king. The insurgents were defeated by Assurdaninpal's younger brother, Shamshi-Adad, who went on to succeed Shalmaneser in 823 BC, but the incessant disharmony among the nobility had weakened the government considerably. The situation worsened during the Eighth Century BC, as successive kings gradually lost their authority over the Assyrian people. In the end, after an ill-omened eclipse of the sun in 763 BC, the monarchy was crippled by another revolt and witnessed the secession of the remaining vassal territories.

XXV

By the time Assyria recovered, the dynamics of the Near East had changed once again. The principal development during the Assyrian decline was the rise of Urartu, an ambitious kingdom founded on the shores of Lake Van in the Armenian highlands. The Urartians were descendants of the Hurrians, who had formed the bulk of the Mitannian Empire, and they occupied large fortified cities that were well equipped with iron. Under the auspices of King Argistis, the Urartian army extended their territory into the Taurus Mountains, reaching the source of the Euphrates. Many of the Neo-Hittite kingdoms fell as the Urartians advanced in the west and a number of vassal states were formed. By the middle of the Eighth Century BC, during the reign of King Sarduri II, Urartu had become the dominant state in the Near East and controlled the trade routes to Anatolia and the Mediterranean.

Faced with the mounting threat of a strong and ambitious enemy just across its borders, Assyria's very existence was at stake and time was running out to recover and respond. Fortunately for the Assyrians, events turned in their favour in 744 BC when the ailing royal family was overthrown and a new dynasty rose to power under the methodical leadership of Tiglath-Pileser III. Reforms were initiated to prevent internal revolts, with the most powerful provinces divided into smaller administrative units and several government posts awarded to eunuchs to circumvent mistrust and escalating rivalries between the noble families. The military was reformed as well, with the generals forced to share their command, while a standing army was created so that longer campaigns could be fought throughout the year, often when enemy soldiers were busy harvesting their land. This paved the way for the army to occupy conquered territories and for centrally appointed governors to rule them as provinces.

Assyria was a strict military state, built upon the core virtues of strength and discipline. Conscription remained in force and those who did not form part of the professional standing army were required to abandon their farms and report for duty when called upon. The Assyrians possessed a vast collection of iron weaponry, dwarfing the resources of their rivals. They also developed formidable battering rams and were the undisputed masters of siege warfare. The army consisted of cavalrymen and charioteers, supported by some of the swiftest horses in the Near East, while hordes of infantrymen, augmented by mercenaries and auxiliaries from vassal states, were armed with swords and spears or bows and arrows, and were renowned for charging the enemy lines with irresistible force.

The revitalised Assyrians marched across the Euphrates, easily defeating the Aramean and Neo-Hittite kingdoms that stood in their way. Tiglath-Pileser showed no hesitation in defeating Urartian vassals in the region and even forced their king, Sarduri III, to flee from battle as he tried to come to the rescue. Yet these campaigns were far from reckless acts of war; it soon became clear that the strategy was not just to plunder foreign states, but to take advantage of the profitable trading network in the west. The obvious target was Phoenicia, and during the first two years of his reign, Tiglath-Pileser invaded the Phoenician cities and ensured that a substantial portion of their trading profits were diverted to the Assyrian treasury. The Phoenicians were not only required to pay annual tribute to the Assyrian king, but they also had to send fixed quantities of their products, including timber, textiles and animal skins. The Assyrians were rapidly monopolising the economic output of the west.

Tiglath-Pileser was successful in the east as well, where new provinces were established beyond the Zagros Mountains for the first time, despite the lively presence of the Medes. In Babylonia he benefited from political unrest as opposition factions invited him to displace an Aramean usurper who had seized the throne. Assisted by many admiring Babylonians, he marched into the city and symbolically took the hand of Marduk at the New Year ceremony in 729 BC, claiming the historic title 'King of Sumer and Akkad'. The only major prize which eluded him was the conquest of Urartu, as although he reached the capital, Tushpa, he failed to find a way through the city's defences. However, his successor, Sargon II, maintained an aggressive stance against the Urartians and pillaged the holy city of Musasir. The defeat was such a devastating blow that the king took his own life in shame. Although Sargon did not go on to conquer the kingdom, he had done enough to suppress the threat. Urartu was eventually destroyed by the Cimmerians; a nomadic tribe of warriors from southern Russia.

The Assyrians had once more become the leading force in the Near East and they commemorated the foundation of a new empire with a flurry of monumental building work, financed by tribute and taxes from conquered territories. A vast array of goods were transported back to Assyria, including precious metals, cattle and slaves, while princesses and fair maidens were sent to the royal palace for the king's pleasure. In contrast, the impoverished inhabitants of the vassal territories faced the ignominy of being stripped of their wealth and having to pay tribute to a foreign king. Some societies lost their autonomy completely and became provinces, directly ruled by an Assyrian governor.

The Assyrians were invariably unwelcome and local rebellions were commonplace, despite the brutal response they received. If the people were spared the horrors of torture and impalement, the unpitying policy of mass deportation was invoked, with entire populations forced to walk long distances to their new homes, often bound in chains. This was intended as a punishment for the rebels and a warning to other vassals, but it also provided the manpower for building new cities and creating farmland in distant regions. In total, over four million people were forcibly removed from their homelands during the long and merciless Assyrian hegemony in the Near East.

XXVI

The century of Assyrian imperial rule beginning in 721 BC was marked by the reigns of four powerful kings, the first of which was the aforementioned Sargon II. To safeguard Assyria's stranglehold on the Near East, Sargon was obliged to overcome the opposition of Egypt and Elam, both of which offered support and encouragement to rebel forces in the Assyrian vassal states. Demonstrating similar military prowess to his namesake from the Third Millennium BC, Sargon recorded decisive victories over these troublesome adversaries and exacted tribute from their kings; the first time Egypt had been subjected to tributary status. Further campaigns were mounted in the west, where the land of the Israelites had long since been divided into two kingdoms: Israel and Judah. When the King of Israel brazenly resisted the payment of tribute, Sargon seized the capital city of Samaria and deported the ten tribes that inhabited the kingdom. The tribes disappeared forever, never returning to their homeland. In contrast, the King of Judah took a more humble approach and paid the tribute that was demanded of him, thus ensuring the survival of his people and their capital, Jerusalem.

By 710 BC, the majority of the Near East had either been conquered or subdued. The notable exception was Babylonia, where the people cast aside their differences to form an anti-Assyrian resistance under Marduk-apla-iddina, chief of a marsh-dwelling tribe known as the Chaldeans. Unperturbed by this new threat, Sargon marched purposefully to Babylon and compelled Marduk-apla-iddina to withdraw to his ancestral home in Sealand. To ensure there would be no reprisals, the Assyrian army pursued him and burned his fortress to the ground. With nowhere else to hide, the

Chaldean was forced into submission although, rather surprisingly, his life was spared. Having cast aside yet another enemy, the conquest of Babylonia was the crowning glory of Sargon. Tribute flooded into Assyria from provinces, vassals and fearful rulers of unconquered lands. The Assyrian army seemed to be inescapable and the vast empire it created was the largest the world had ever seen.

Meanwhile, beyond the borders of the empire, new forces were beginning to make themselves known. In Anatolia, the Phrygians integrated with the Mushki people, who were ruled by the legendary King Mita; better known by his Greek name, Midas. During his reign, the Phrygians accumulated substantial wealth from the Anatolian gold mines, hence the myth that everything Midas touched turned to gold. As the Eighth Century BC drew to a close, the Phrygians were invaded by the Cimmerians; the tribe of nomadic warriors from beyond the Caucasus Mountains who had already conquered the Urartians. The Cimmerians had been driven out of their homeland by their fearsome neighbours, the Scythians, who eventually followed them into the Near East. Having laid waste to Urartu, the Cimmerians continued in a westerly direction along the southern shoreline of the Black Sea and into the heart of Anatolia.

With his kingdom under attack, Midas asked for assistance from Sargon, who willingly led his army into central Anatolia to confront the Cimmerians in 705 BC. The ensuing events were most unexpected. Perhaps taking their barbarous enemies for granted, the Assyrians were heavily defeated and Sargon himself was killed in battle. Midas escaped, but the Cimmerians followed him to the Phrygian capital, Gordion, and forced him to commit suicide. The defeat of the Phrygians chiefly benefitted the rival kingdom of Lydia, which blossomed around the city of Sardis under King Gyges in the early Seventh Century BC. The Lydians soon found themselves under attack by the Cimmerians as well, leading to the death of

Gyges and the capture of Sardis, but a generation later they avenged the defeat and displaced the Cimmerians as the dominant power in Anatolia.

Back in Assyria, Sargon was succeeded by his son, Sennacherib. The new king's first priority was to rebuild the ancient city of Nineveh and transform it into the capital of an empire. The city was graced with new streets and market squares, two citadels and a grandiose palace befitting a supreme monarch. This was the most obvious demonstration of Assyrian wealth amidst a sustained period of pride and prosperity; a single military defeat in Anatolia did not change that. However, as the conceited and oppressive nature of imperial rule provoked a series of rebellions in the vassal territories, Sennacherib and his successors were left with the tiresome and unrelenting task of maintaining control of the empire. It is likely that Assyria's constant struggle to reassert its authority influenced the later empires of Persia and Rome, both of whom tended to show more leniency to the inhabitants of conquered lands in order to encourage their peaceful acquiescence.

Resistance against Assyrian rule was most vociferous in Babylonia, where the Chaldean insurgent, Marduk-apla-iddina, returned from exile and, supported by the Elamites and Arameans, marched into Babylon, proclaiming himself the rightful ruler of the city. Sennacherib reacted in the expected manner by leading his troops into battle and defeating the rebels on the outskirts of Kish. Marduk-apla-iddina was again forced to flee into the marshlands with the Assyrian army on his tail. As Sennacherib was evidently not going to spare his life in the same manner as his father, the wretched Chaldean hurriedly gathered together the statues of his gods and the bones of his ancestors and sailed out to sea, leaving his family and followers behind. He was never caught, but died in exile. Sennacherib immediately placed a puppet ruler on the Babylonian throne and deported over two hundred thousand Chaldean prisoners to Assyria in retribution.

He may have extinguished the flames of another revolt, but Sennacherib was growing tired of policing southern Mesopotamia and in 694 BC he embarked upon a more aggressive campaign with the primary goal of securing uninhibited access to the Gulf. Yet although he plundered many cities, the Babylonians and Elamites put up a stubborn united front and even managed to capture the king's eldest son, Assur-nadin-shumi, who was taken in chains to Elam and never seen again. With the momentum on their side, the Babylonians sensed a rare opportunity to attack and quickly gathered as much gold as they could from the Temple of Marduk to pay the Elamite king for his ongoing support. The allied army amounted to sizeable force and in 691 BC they came close to defeating Sennacherib at the Battle of Halule, near the Assyrian border. However a decisive victory eluded them and instead left the hapless Babylonians facing the wrath of an angry Assyrian king.

Already exasperated by the loss of his son, the allied attack was the final straw for Sennacherib, and in 689 BC he exerted the ultimate revenge by ordering his generals to destroy the famous city of Babylon. Unmoved by centuries of Babylonian cultural influence on his homeland, the Assyrian king watched from a distance as his soldiers massacred the inhabitants, burned their houses and temples to the ground and flooded the land until there was nothing left but water, ashes and dust. When the devastation was complete, the statue of Marduk and all the other Babylonian treasures were transported in their entirety to Assur.

The surviving Babylonians may have taken some consolation from the fate of Sennacherib, who was murdered in cold blood by his two eldest sons in 681 BC. They were upset because he had chosen their younger brother, Esarhaddon, as heir to the throne. Esarhaddon had been driven into exile because of the jealously of his brothers, but in the commotion following his father's death, he returned as the people's champion and took his place on the throne. The new king had many of the attributes his father lacked, such as compassion and political tact, and his first priority was to rebuild the city of Babylon which had been so recklessly demolished. It took his entire reign to complete the task, but in doing so the new king endeared himself to the Babylonian people and was rewarded with their eternal gratitude and obedience.

The key to Esarhaddon's success lay in his firm, but more considered approach to foreign policy. He was certainly not afraid to show his tougher side, as demonstrated following a revolt in the Phoenician city of Sidon, where the king was beheaded, the population enslaved, and the territory awarded to the rival city of Tyre. He also repelled a dangerous threat from the north, where the barbaric Scythians had belligerently crossed the Taurus Mountains. Undaunted, Esarhaddon promptly launched an offensive in the region and forced the Scythians to retreat towards Anatolia. Once they were out of harm's way, he opted for diplomatic measures instead, epitomised by the marriage of his daughter to a Scythian prince. Elsewhere, he made inroads into Median territory and applied enough pressure on Elam to ensure the succession of a prince who was friendly to Assyria.

Esarhaddon effectively combined ambition and prudence and proved remarkably successful in advancing Assyrian interests throughout the empire. With little to occupy his armies in the Near East, he was free to embark upon his greatest and boldest mission: the invasion and conquest of Egypt. In 671 BC, having been assured of the neutrality of the Arabs in the Syrian Desert, Esarhaddon led his army into the delta and conquered the city of Memphis in just half a day, forcing the incumbent king, Taharqo, to flee to his Nubian homeland. The kingdom of Egypt, once the mightiest in the ancient world, was henceforth divided into twenty principalities, with the native rulers required to swear allegiance to the Assyrian king. Esarhaddon exultantly returned home to Assyria; however just two years later he was compelled to journey back to Egypt when word reached him that Taharqo was marching towards the delta with a newly assembled army. The Assyrian king confidently set out across the Near East but fell ill along the way and died before he reached Egyptian territory. It was an unfortunate end to a fruitful reign.

The last in the line of great Assyrian kings was Assurbanipal, a determined and popular monarch who came to power in 668 BC without any of the problems that had hampered his father's succession. To curtail the risk of civil war, his elder brother, Shamash-shum-ukin, was crowned King of Babylon at the same time; a decision which also served to appease the Babylonian people by giving them a veneer of independence. Assurbanipal was not a courageous king, refusing to go into battle himself and leaving the campaigning to his generals. Like his ancestors, he enjoyed taking part in lion hunts, but instead of boldly riding after them through the open fields and forests, he insisted that the lions were to be caged and wounded before their release. Rather than taking part in military campaigns, he devoted much of his time to building a grand library in Nineveh, which included an enormous collection of works from Assyria and Babylonia, ranging from scientific lists and tables to religious and literary texts such the infamous *Epic of Gilgamesh*. Whether he spent much time in the library is doubtful, but he certainly seems to have found it more appealing than risking his life on the battlefield.

Nevertheless, to preserve the wealth of the royal treasury, it was important that Assyria continued to suppress foreign states and Assurbanipal wasted little time in dispatching his army to Egypt to continue his father's mission. The Assyrians defeated the rebels at Memphis, but Taharqo escaped yet again and headed south. Assurbanipal briefly considered a pursuit, but on hearing of a planned revolt among the native rulers in the delta, he changed his mind and appointed a puppet leader, Necho, to keep the peace. Taharqo died soon afterwards, but his cousin, Tantamani, promptly sailed to Memphis and defeated Necho in battle. Angered by this episode, Assurbanipal ordered his commanders to seize the delta once again, but insisted that this time they were to pursue the rebels all the way to Thebes. The Assyrian generals heeded his words and much to the Egyptians' dismay, the majestic city of Thebes, supposedly under the eternal protection of the gods, was sacked and plundered by foreigners.

This was a bitter psychological blow, but the Egyptians refused to give up their independence easily and in 655 BC, Necho's son, Psamtik, recruited a number of Greek and Lydian mercenaries to help drive out the Assyrians from Egypt. Under normal circumstances, Assurbanipal would surely have retaliated immediately, but on this occasion he was preoccupied by a major crisis in Mesopotamia. His envious brother, Shamash-shum-ukin, had conspired to bring an end to Assyrian domination by orchestrating a synchronised attack on Assyria by the other major forces of the Near East, including the Babylonians, Chaldeans, Elamites, Lydians, Phoenicians, Philistines, Jews and Arabs. An assault on this scale would doubtless have been fatal for the Assyrians, but Assurbanipal discovered the plot before it was put into action and unleashed the might of the Assyrian army against his treacherous brother. After four years of fighting and a prolonged siege of Babylon, the starving Babylonians, ravaged by disease and reduced to cannibalism, finally surrendered in 648 BC. With all hope exhausted, Shamash-shum-ukin despairingly threw himself into the flames of his burning palace.

With victory assured, Assurbanipal smelled blood and launched reprisal attacks against the Arabs and Elamites, whom he judged to have been the most enthusiastic about the conspiracy. The former were quickly subdued, but a harsher fate awaited the latter. Ever since the first empires were formed in the Third Millennium BC, the Elamites had been a constant thorn in the side of the Mesopotamian kings, and on this occasion they had gone too far. In 639 BC, Assurbanipal's army bludgeoned its way through Elamite territory, set fire to Susa and the other towns and cities, covered the fields in salt and deported the population on mass. Elam continued to exist as a weak and fragmented state for another century but never again emerged as a threat to Mesopotamia.

When all was said and done, the merciless Assurbanipal had preserved the status of the empire, but at the expense of thousands of lives and some of the most magnificent cities in the ancient world. In doing so, he was simply following a trend set by his predecessors, whose overriding policy was to subdue foreign states so that the Assyrian royals and nobles could immerse themselves in military glory, power and wealth. A fundamental part of this strategy was to ensure that the rest of the world was incessantly shackled by fear. This was achieved by shocking brutality against conquered states, where men were routinely tortured, blinded and beheaded, with their heads put on display as a warning to others, while the women were beaten, raped and sold into slavery with their children, to such an extent that the price of a slave eventually became less than that of a camel. If anyone dared to hide behind their city walls, their houses, farmland and orchards were obliterated, swiftly ending any hopes of riding out the storm.

The shocking consequences of resisting the imperial army encouraged many communities to surrender without a fight, but also resulted in widespread hatred of the Assyrian regime throughout the Near East. The Assyrian kings may have been oblivious to the problem, but their decadent and repressive policies were putting a tremendous strain on government resources due to the unremitting need for the army to quash rebellions and elicit taxes in foreign lands. The situation was worsened by endless campaigning, which significantly reduced the manpower of the army and left the surviving soldiers feeling exhausted. As imperious as the empire may have seemed, it was actually growing weaker by the day. In spite of Assyria's military victories, Egypt had regained its independence, Lydia openly supported rebellions in the vassal states, and the Phoenicians were no longer able to transfer as much wealth to Nineveh as they had lost control of Mediterranean trade to the Greeks.

More worryingly, beyond the borders of the empire, there were other enemies who could no longer be kept at arm's length. The most dangerous threat was from the Medes, who had amassed a substantial army in the east and were patiently waiting for an opportunity to attack. Their first attempt, led by King Phraortes, ended in failure, but a generation later, an army commanded by his son, Cyaxares, entered Assyria itself and laid siege to Nineveh. This probably took place in 630 BC. The Assyrians appear to have been spared because of a surprise attack on the Medes by the Scythians, but it was clear for all to see that the great power of Assyria had become a spent force. The ageing Assurbanipal died in 627 BC and nominally left the empire to his son, Assur-etil-ilani, but in reality he left nothing but a poisoned chalice. The age of Assyrian domination was over.

XXVII

As news of the Median invasion spread across the Near East, the provinces and vassal states took the opportunity to free themselves from the Assyrian yoke. The cities of Phoenicia and Judah were located far enough from Nineveh to gain their independence without a struggle. Closer to home, fighting took place in Babylon, where Assurbanipal's younger son, Sin-shar-ishkun, was forced to surrender the city to Nabopolassar, leader of the Chaldeans. Wounded by his loss, Sin-shar-ishkun withdrew to Nineveh and decided to take up arms against his brother instead, eventually defeating him in battle to seize the Assyrian throne for himself. He then returned to Babylon to face Nabopolassar, but was repelled again by the Chaldeans. Nabopolassar was crowned king in Babylon with popular support, having avenged the defeat of the former Chaldean hero, Marduk-apla-iddina, and the thousands of his countrymen who had been deported by the Assyrians at the beginning of the century. The new regime, later known as the Neo-Babylonian dynasty, led to a renaissance of Babylonian culture as the inhabitants of the illustrious city enjoyed their independence for one last time.

On the other side of the Zagros Mountains, the Medes had strengthened their kingdom around the city of Ecbatana and were becoming more ambitious under the leadership of Cyaxares. The Medes, together with their near neighbours, the Persians, were Indo-European migrants who had arrived from the east at the beginning of the Iron Age. Although they paid tribute to the Assyrians from as early as the Ninth Century BC, the mountainous border between them afforded some protection from Assyrian raids and allowed them the freedom to expand their territories. When the

Persians migrated southwards to inherit the former Elamite province of Anshan and then further south to claim the land of Parsa, the Medes remained as the main threat to Assyria's eastern borders.

Herodotus tells us that following the surprise attack by the Scythians, Cyaxares had to pay tribute to the Scythian chieftains, but freed himself from this obligation when he murdered the leaders while they were getting drunk at a banquet. With the Scythians deprived of their command, the Medes were once again free to enter the west. Prior to this episode, the Scythian cavalrymen had embarked upon a series of raids across the Near East, exploiting defenceless towns and cities that had been abandoned by Assyria. They may even have entered Egypt, had it not been for the intervention of Psamtik, who bribed them to turn back. Unsurprisingly, when the Medes advanced across the Zagros Mountains, the Egyptians feared another approach by a hostile enemy and were persuaded to accept Sin-shar-ishkun's offer of an alliance with Assyria, despite centuries of antagonism between their respective countries.

Unfortunately for the Assyrians, Egyptian aid arrived too late. In 615 BC, the Medes invaded Assyria again and seized Assur in the following year. Nabopolassar and his Chaldean army were informed of the Median advance and hurriedly marched up the Euphrates, but were too late to take part in the battle. Instead they met the Median generals in the vanquished city and agreed to an alliance, sealed by the marriage of Nabopolassar's son, Nebuchadnezzar, with Cyaxares' daughter, Amytis. Three years later, a coalition consisting of Medes, Chaldeans and Scythians set up camp outside Nineveh, and following a three month siege, the Assyrians were finally defeated. Sin-shar-ishkun was said to have died in the city as the buildings burned around him. His successor, Assur-uballit II, fled to the west and made a final stand in the Syrian city of Harran, supported at last by Assyria's Egyptian allies, but they were soon made to flee by the Median army and by 610 BC the Assyrian resistance was over.

The Medes and Chaldeans divided the Assyrian homeland amongst themselves and revelled in the final defeat of a cruel and monstrous empire. Still haunted by vivid memories of Assyrian brutality, the Babylonians tore down the statues of their chief tormentors, Sennacherib and Assurbanipal, and cut out their eyes and ears. Once the defacing was complete, the great palaces were destroyed and the cities of Nineveh and Nimrud were reduced to huge mounds of earth. Presumably for religious reasons, the holy city of Assur was spared from total destruction and its inhabitants were eventually permitted to return. With the Chaldeans content to remain in the south, Cyaxares and his Median army began to dominate northern Mesopotamia, inheriting the remnants of Urartu, driving the Scythians back into the Caucasus Mountains and occupying cities all over Syria. They also confronted the Lydians in Anatolia, although according to Herodotus this encounter was brought to a halt by an eclipse of the sun which prompted the two sides to agree a peace treaty.

Meanwhile, following their defeat at Harran, the Egyptians proceeded to seize the western territories that had only recently gained their independence from Assyria, including the Phoenician city-states and the Kingdom of Judah. They also held the strategic city of Carchemish on the western bank of the Euphrates. This infuriated the Babylonians, who had finally rid themselves of Assyrian overlordship, only to be denied control of the Mediterranean trade route by the accursed Egyptians. Nabopolassar was growing old by this time and the task of expelling the Egyptians fell to his son, Nebuchadnezzar. In 605 BC, the young prince bravely attacked Carchemish and overcame the Egyptians in a bloody battle before pursuing them into Palestine.

Nebuchadnezzar was still in pursuit of the Egyptian army when he received news of his father's death and without delay he returned to Babylon to become king. Once the formalities were over, he marched back to the Levant as King Nebuchadnezzar II to flaunt his power and collect tribute from the Syrians, Phoenicians, Philistines and Judeans, all of whom were resentful towards their new oppressors, having only recently freed themselves of their obligations to Assyria. Indeed, feelings against Babylon were running so high that in 597 BC, King Jehoiakim of Judah impudently decided to stop paying tribute. The response was swift and unpitying: the Babylonian army stormed into Jerusalem, murdered the king and took thousands of its leading men captive, including his son, Jehoiachin. The invading soldiers then proceeded to raid the Jewish temples and carried the spoils back to Babylon.

With Jehoiachin detained in the palace at Babylon, his uncle, Zedekiah, was permitted to rule the remaining population in Jerusalem. However, a decade later he fatefully decided to switch allegiance to the Egyptians, who remained active in the region and were in the process of reducing a number of Palestinian cities to vassalage. Nebuchadnezzar was incensed and dispatched a huge army, threatening enough for the Egyptians to abandon their new vassal states, and his forces soon arrived unopposed at the walls of Jerusalem. In 586 BC, after an eighteen month siege that left the inhabitants disease-ridden and starving, the Babylonian army entered the city, looted the palace and temples (including the holy temple of King Solomon) and burned them to the ground. Zedekiah escaped but was captured and made to watch the execution of his sons before being blinded and led away in chains to Babylon. Thousands more Judeans were deported to Babylonia. Just as the Israelites had been vanquished and exiled by the Assyrians, so their Jewish kinsmen suffered the same fate at the hands of the Babylonians. After these devastating events it was only the enduring appeal of their religious ideas that preserved the identity of the Jews.

Nebuchadnezzar had unfinished business in the west and proceeded to lay siege to the Phoenician city of Tyre, whose king,

Ithobalus, had followed the dangerous precedent set by Zedekiah. The Tyrians put up a stubborn defence, aided by supplies shipped in from the sea, but after thirteen years of defiance, the city fell. The Babylonian king also set his sights on Egypt, but after a series of skirmishes, the two sides agreed to fix a border between them. With or without Egypt, Babylon presided over an empire and Nebuchadnezzar's work was done. Tribute was collected from the vassal states and for the first time this included actual money; the earliest gold and silver coinage had been minted at the turn of the century by the Lydians.

Having won their freedom and gained vast quantities of riches from conquered lands and via the trade routes that had been reopened to them, the Babylonian people commemorated the dawn of a golden era by embellishing their famous city with renewed vigour and pride. Inside the royal court, nobles from Media, Syria, Phoenicia and Anatolia intermingled with the Babylonian elite, creating a pulsating multicultural community which adhered to the ancient and respected culture of southern Mesopotamia, even preserving Akkadian as the official language of the state. The nostalgic Babylonians looked back upon their heritage with fondness and encouraged their subjects to do likewise. As the city flourished once more, the dark days of Assyrian oppression were soon banished from their memories.

In the time of Nebuchadnezzar, the city of Babylon had a population of over a hundred thousand, most of whom lived in houses made of mud brick or reeds, often surrounded by palm trees. Bisected by the Euphrates, the city was protected by two great walls which contained the royal palace and more than a thousand temples, including the *Esagila*: the temple of Marduk. Eight gates were positioned on the inner walls, of which the most outstanding was the Ishtar Gate; an extravagantly decorated edifice adorned with blue tiles and colourful images of lions, dragons and bulls. In the centre of the city, rising spectacularly above the skyline, was the Tower of

Babel; an enormous ziggurat of at least seven tiers which may have been up to a hundred metres high. Yet perhaps the most famous of all the marvels in Babylon were the stunning Hanging Gardens, considered by classical observers to be one of the Seven Wonders of the World. According to one source, the gardens were erected by Nebuchadnezzar for his wife, Amytis, to remind her of the mountains in her Median homeland.

The renaissance of Babylon was epitomised by the New Year festival, *Akitu*, which marked the annual congregation of the gods to decide the fate of the world for another year. The event lasted eleven or twelve days and began with a procession of statues of the gods from the other cities of Babylonia which were transported along the Euphrates to stand alongside the golden statue of Marduk in the *Esagila*. The Babylonians believed that only the gods could decide the destiny of mankind and were genuinely nervous about the outcome. On the fifth day, the king entered the temple and was ritually stripped of his insignia and slapped by a priest to symbolise his inferiority to the gods. He was then made to assure the people that he was free from sin. On the ninth day, the king symbolically took the hand of Marduk and led the statue in a chariot across the city, through the Ishtar Gate, to a temple by the river. This signalled to the public that the gods had ruled in their favour. Amidst much celebration, the festival ended with a huge banquet, accompanied by wine, music and prayers.

One of the greatest Mesopotamian kings and the last to rule an empire, Nebuchadnezzar eventually died of illness in 562 BC. He was succeeded by his son, Amel-Marduk, who did not endear himself to his people and was soon killed in a revolt led by his brother-in-law, Neriglissar. The latter ruled for three years before leaving the throne to his own son, Labashi-Marduk. Despite his tender age, the Babylonian nobles sensed the young king was a wicked man and conspired to kill him before he could make his mark. One of the conspirators, Nabonidus, then ascended the throne in 555 BC. An intriguing character, Nabonidus was already in his sixties when he became king and was extremely devoted to his mother, Adad-guppi, who lived until she was 104. Throughout her life she had vehemently worshipped the moon god, Sin, and Nabonidus decided to respect her wishes by continuing to hold Sin in high regard and adorning his temples, to a greater extent even than the temples of Marduk. He also made his daughter the High Priestess of the moon god at Ur; an ancient title that had not been invoked for many years.

The Babylonian nobles and the priesthood of Marduk were already aware that Nabonidus was not of royal blood and his religious inclinations quickly turned them against him. Their agitation grew as the king's behaviour went from the unorthodox to the bizarre. In 552 BC he suddenly abandoned the city for self-imposed exile in the Arabian Desert, leaving his son, Belshazzar, in charge. Ignoring impassioned pleas for his return, Nabonidus remained in the desert for ten years, resulting in the abandonment of the New Year festival, much to the anguish of the Babylonian people. When he finally returned, he caused further consternation by converting several of Marduk's temples into sanctuaries for Sin. As rumours circulated that the king was either a heretic or insane, it was clear that something needed to be done to preserve the dignity of the city.

Throughout the troubled reign of Nabonidus, an ambitious foreign king was busy earning the respect and admiration of both his own people and those abroad. His name was Cyrus, the infamous ruler of the Persians, whose kingdom had already transcended the Median Empire and was steadily consuming territories across the Near East. Far from being a bloodthirsty oppressor like the Assyrian kings, Cyrus was courteous and respectful to conquered peoples and their customs. Portraying himself as a great liberator, his methods were in stark contrast to the erratic policies of Nabonidus, and the Babylonian nobility and priesthood actively encouraged the people to accept the rule of Cyrus, mainly so that the pre-eminence of Marduk could be restored. In 539 BC, their prayers were answered when the Persians invaded Babylon. Nabonidus instructed Belshazzar to raise an army to defend the city but he was soon killed in battle and his troops were routed by the Persians. Nabonidus fled but was eventually captured and executed, leaving Cyrus to enter the gates of Babylon unopposed and march through the city streets to popular acclaim.

The people of Babylonia celebrated the survival of their traditions and willingly consented to Persian rule. Yet this was also the moment when they lost their independence forever. The Persian conquest of Babylon signalled the dawn of a new age, in which the affairs of the Near East, Egypt and beyond would be dominated by the Persian kings and their governors. In fact it would take the determination and courage of a resurgent Greece to challenge Persian ambitions in what was to become an epic struggle between the civilizations of east and west. This was the beginning of the classical age; a celebrated era in which humanity made even greater strides by creating societies that were habitually embellished with cultural and intellectual brilliance.

XXVIII

The inhabitants of the ancient Near East, Nile Valley and Mediterranean resolutely believed that they lived in the centre of the universe and, with the exception of a few adventurous merchants who were aware of the Indus Valley through their trading contacts, they were oblivious to the other civilizations that coexisted thousands of miles to the east and west. However by the Sixth Century BC, these distant societies had already left complex histories behind them, shaped by deeply engrained cultural traditions that would endure long after their first tentative relations with so-called western civilization. In the case of the Americas, this initial contact would not take place until barely five hundred years before our own time. In India and China, natural geographical barriers and the sheer distance between these regions and their contemporary civilizations would preserve diversity even when cross-cultural interactions became more frequent.

Of these other worlds, only the Indians shared a degree of cultural heritage with the Near East because of the Indo-European migrations which took place at about the same time that distantly related tribes were first entering Greece. By then, a wide-reaching civilization had already been attained by the native inhabitants. The first Indian communities were located in the valley of the Indus; the north-western area of the subcontinent. Agriculture was established by c.6,000 BC and permanent settlements appeared three thousand years later, in the early Bronze Age. Sheltered by a mountainous frontier that separated the plains of the Indus from the furthest expanses of the Near East, the Indus tribes had minimal contact with the other civilizations of the ancient world and developed in their own distinctive way. At this time the land of India only comprised the plains of the Indus; the Ganges had not yet been penetrated, while the dangerous jungles of the southern peninsula, teeming with elephants, tigers and crocodiles, were inhospitable and the people who lived there remained isolated from their neighbours.

In contrast with the civilizations of Mesopotamia and Egypt, very little is known about the political administration or religious ideas of the earliest Indian cities. It is uncertain whether they formed part of a unified state, while the identities of their kings and other historical characters have not been revealed. Nevertheless, archaeological evidence has confirmed that the earliest cities appeared in c.2,600 BC, with the principal sites being Harappa in the north and Mohenjo-Daro, four hundred miles further south. The cities were methodically designed, with rectangular blocks of brick houses divided by wide streets and flanked by a sophisticated drainage system. Each city was constructed around a citadel, which enclosed public buildings such as the temple and granary. They were maintained by surpluses produced from the surrounding farmland and through the export of fine crafts made in the workshops, including precious beads of gold, copper and ivory.

Early trade links were established between Mesopotamian merchants and traders from the mysterious land of Meluhha, which is commonly believed to have been the Akkadian name for the Indus Valley. Although the journey would have been long and arduous by land or sea, it appears that the first Indian exports reached Mesopotamia during the Third Millennium BC. The early contact between these distant societies leads to the possibility that the Sumerian model of civilization travelled in the other direction, potentially providing the impetus for the original Indian towns and cities. Yet even if the Indian people were inspired by ideas emanating from the Near East, they fashioned their own distinguishing styles in everything from house-building to painting, pottery and writing. As time went on, the natural barriers and infrequent contact between the two regions enabled Indian societies to develop in virtual isolation from the rest of the civilized world.

During the early Second Millennium BC, the Indus Valley civilization entered a period of decline, probably as a result of flooding and deforestation which damaged the economy and severely restricted trade. After 1750 BC, with the influence of the cities having all but disappeared, the autonomy of the native Indians also came to an end when migrants from the west began to arrive in India and impose their authority upon the native people. The new arrivals were yet another branch of Indo-Europeans; the linguistic group whose ancestry was shared by a range of tribes, including the Hittites, Kassites, Greeks and Persians. The tribes that migrated to Persia and India respectively described themselves as *Airiia* and *Arya* and became known to future Europeans as the Aryans. Much later, during the Nineteenth and Twentieth Centuries AD, the concept of Aryanism was misapplied to all speakers of the Indo-European languages, usually with racial connotations.

Contrary to the theories of some historians over the years, it does not appear that the Aryans embarked upon a single mass migration into India; instead the evidence suggests that they gradually infiltrated the Indus Valley in a series of small-scale migrations. They entered the country upon horses and chariots as warriors and pastoralists, but as they travelled across wide expanses of fertile land, they progressively took up agriculture and settled amongst the existing populations, even incorporating elements of the native languages into their own. Although the cities of Harappa and Mohenjo-Daro lost control of the surrounding farmland at about the same time, there are no indications they were subjected to violence by invaders. In fact, the Aryans, not being used to urban life, may have quickly abandoned or simply ignored the deteriorating cities. In the absence of any central administration from the cities, the Aryan chieftains, the Rajas, assumed control of the villages, and by 1200 BC they held power throughout the Indus Valley.

The Aryans brought with them religious ideas that moulded Indian society and laid the foundations of Hinduism; now the world's third most popular religion, after Christianity and Islam. Aryan beliefs doubtless evolved over thousands of years and were first written down in the language of Sanskrit, forming a series of texts that were collectively known as the *Vedas*. The earliest and most important of these was the *Rig Veda*; a compilation of hymns that revealed the names of the Vedic deities, including Indra, king of the gods, Varuna, god of water, and Agni, god of fire. Intriguingly, some of these deities were also referred to in a treaty between the Hittites and Mitannians in the Fourteenth Century BC, indicating that the dispersed Indo-European tribes shared a religious heritage, presumably deriving from their common ancestral homeland. Indeed, there is also a close relationship between the *Rig Vega* and the *Avesta*; the sacred text of the Persian religion, Zoroastrianism.

Before the *Vedas* were written down, they were memorised and transmitted orally by Aryan priests, the Brahmans, whose religious knowledge gave them exclusive rights to preside over Vedic rituals and sacrifices. The Brahmans devised a strict social hierarchy which divided the people into different castes according to their perceived religious purity. In descending order, the four castes, known as the *varnas*, were the Brahmans (priests), Kshatriyas (aristocrats or warriors), Vaishyas (farmers or merchants) and Shudras (labourers or slaves). A fifth group, the Untouchables, lived in poverty and were considered to be impure and polluted. In fact, only the first three castes were allowed to participate in rituals, while the remainder were scorned and left to follow their own religions. The people were also arranged into numerous *jatis*, usually on the basis of occupation. When new groups were encountered, they were absorbed within the appropriate *varna* and *jati* depending on their status, language and role within the community. Initially there were clear divisions between the *aryas* (Aryans) and the *dasas* (foreigners) as well, but as they intermingled, many of the latter came to be respected by the Brahmans and were assimilated into the higher castes. From the outset, the caste system was hereditary and allowed little room for intermarriage or social mobility, particularly in respect of the *varnas*.

While the Brahmans maintained authority over religious matters and issues relating to caste, military operations were controlled by the Rajas, whose objectives were to protect the land and carry out raids in neighbouring communities, chiefly to acquire livestock and booty. The Brahmans orchestrated ritual sacrifices in which they were believed to make contact with the gods and bestow divinity upon the Rajas, legitimising their rule over the people. After each sacrifice had been completed, the Raja would present gifts to twelve Kshatriyas or Vaishyas, usually from the proceeds of his military ventures. He would then release a horse to roam freely across the countryside, henceforth claiming all the land that it came into contact with. Of course, the Raja had to be sufficiently wealthy and powerful to take part in these rituals and it was only after adequately proving himself to the Brahmans that divine status would be conferred.

The lives of ordinary people in Vedic society were centred on the family, who resided together in mud brick houses and often shared the same living space as their animals. When they were not craft-working or farming the land, they would prepare meals, sing, dance and gamble, usually by playing dice games. Education was open to the three higher castes, although it was mainly the Brahmans that engaged in study. The Brahmans and Rajas administered the law and generally invoked harsher punishments if the offender was a Shudra or an Untouchable. That said, punishments were less severe than in most ancient societies; even murderers were sometimes spared death or mutilation and were instead required to pay a penalty of one hundred cows. Under the strict rule of the Brahmans, Vedic society was highly regulated and some disillusioned men were induced to seek an alternative lifestyle of wandering, meditation and yoga, where they were free to contemplate philosophy and achieve a higher spiritual state. Needless to say, such activities were limited to the few aristocrats who could afford to do so.

By the Seventh Century BC, Aryan culture had penetrated the jungles to the south and east, and the centre of Indian civilization had shifted from the Indus to the Ganges. Trade between the two regions was broadly an exchange of fine crafts and beads from the east for horses and wool from the west. The Indian world had entered the Iron Age, probably through trading contacts with the Persians, enabling farmers and craftsmen to increase the rate of production and therefore the wealth of their communities. As Indian society flourished, villages became towns and the Rajas consolidated their position through hereditary succession, ruling increasingly large kingdoms with more defined boundaries. There were known to be sixteen such kingdoms in northern India and rivalries between them resulted in great wars, characterised by the use of stampeding elephants. The spoils of war were enjoyed by the ruling families and of course the Brahmans, whose status remained as important and influential as ever.

The Indian kingdoms may have dominated the plains of the Indus and Ganges, but the subcontinent remained exceptionally culturally diverse. Vedic religion and practices were rejected by autonomous communities known as the *Gana-sanghas*, where society was less hierarchical and more introspective. These were located on the fringes of the great kingdoms and later fostered the alternative belief systems of Buddhism and Jainism. Meanwhile, the many tribes who spoke the Dravidian languages in southern India continued to lead primitive lifestyles and remained oblivious to the bustling Aryan societies of the north. With the southern Indian terrain as wild and hostile as ever, this would remain the case for many years to come.

XXIX

Further to the East, beyond the immense and imposing mountain range of the Himalayas, there existed another enigmatic civilization, probably unbeknown to the Indians or anyone from the Near East. First appearing on the plains of the Yellow River in c.1500 BC, Chinese culture blossomed and slowly spread southwards into the valleys of the Yangtze and Xi, forging a national identity that remains unbroken to this day. Agricultural communities have existed in north-eastern China since the middle of the Seventh Millennium BC, but progress was much slower than in the Near East and it was another five thousand years before the appearance of the Chinese Bronze Age and the first traces of civilization. Although it is possible that knowledge of metallurgy was garnered from the west, perhaps indirectly from the Near East via nomadic tribes in Mongolia, the earliest bronze artefacts in China were very different to those from elsewhere and credit for these innovations must be attributed to the native people.

The first Chinese tribe to seize the initiative were the Shang, whose bronze weapons and swift chariots gave them an advantage over their neighbours, enabling them to convert a large area around the Yellow River into their domain. Chinese tradition attests that Cheng Tang of the Shang defeated the prevailing Xia Dynasty, although no evidence has been found to confirm the existence of this earlier regime. In any event, the Shang soon established their authority and after a period of moving their capital between various locations, in the Fourteenth Century BC they settled in the small village of Yin, which rapidly developed into a city and became the hub of the Shang Dynasty for the next two and a half centuries. In the same arbitrary manner as the pharaohs in Egypt, the Shang kings ruled supreme and were given elaborate burials, honoured by both human and animal sacrifices. The remains were buried next to the king in the royal tomb, presumably to serve him in the afterlife.

The Shang kings were highly spiritual leaders who tended to consult oracles before making important decisions, particularly concerning hunting expeditions and warfare. The king would engrave a question onto a tortoise shell or shoulder blade of an ox and then touch it with a hot bronze rod, creating cracks on the surface which would then be interpreted by the king himself or one of his advisors. The answer was said to have been given by one of his royal ancestors, who were worshipped as gods. The remnants of the oracles provide us with the earliest evidence of Chinese writing. Using the same script, scribes were employed in the cities for administrative purposes to regulate the economy and mobilise labour forces for mining, bronze-working, building cities or undertaking military campaigns. From the outset, the Chinese language consisted of ideograms, with each symbol having the same meaning, regardless of how it was pronounced in different dialects. Consequently the spread of the Shang script encouraged a degree of cultural unity among the numerous and diverse Chinese tribes from a very early stage.

The Shang continued to expand their territory in a westerly direction along the Yellow River until they reached the Taihang Mountains. Here their progress was checked by a formidable tribe known as the Zhou, whose own territory had been expanding in the opposite direction. By the middle of the Eleventh Century BC, the overlord of the Shang was King Di Xin, a detestable man who led an immoral lifestyle, forgoing his political responsibilities for drinking parties and orgies, while frequently raising taxes and carrying out grotesque executions on his political rivals. One of his surviving opponents, a military commander by the name of Jiang Ziya, was so perturbed by the king's methods that he fled the Shang kingdom and begged King Wu of the Zhou to permit him to lead an army to overthrow Di Xin. Permission was duly granted and in 1046 BC Jiang Ziya's forces were victorious at the Battle of Muye, enabling Wu to enter the city of Yin and seize control of the Shang kingdom. The mortified Di Xin retreated to the royal palace where he burned himself to death, surrounded by all his treasure.

Having absorbed the Shang Kingdom into his own, King Wu presided over a huge empire, centred on the Wei River (a tributary of the Yellow River) and extending as far as the Yangtze in the south. The main pillars of Shang culture remained, including their system of writing, bronze-working techniques and many of the same rituals, but the Zhou Dynasty enabled the spread of these ideas to many more tribes. Of course it was impossible for the king to oversee all his territories at once and this led to the establishment of a feudal-like system, with fiefs divided among the king's brothers and other members of the royal family. These relatives became powerful lords who also served as military leaders, scholars and priests, and effectively ruled their own small kingdoms. The conduct of the lords was moderated by the principle of *li* ('rules of propriety') which required them to be chivalrous and eternally loyal to the king, raising an army for him if necessary. On occasions, the lords fought between themselves, often with the king taking one side or the other; however most of these battles were on a small scale and were fought for pride rather than the permanent occupation of another fiefdom.

The lives of the Zhou kings and lords were on the whole simple but pleasurable. Aside from fulfilling religious and military functions, they spent most of their time hunting, planning new building projects or relaxing with their concubines, of which there were many. They resided with their fellow aristocrats in the centre of their territories, protected by city walls and surrounded by merchants and more distantly by the peasants who lived on the farmland outside the cities. In contrast to their overlords, the peasants must have lived wearisome lives, working long and hard for scant reward. Little is known about their unfortunate existence, which was probably akin to slavery. They may have worshipped their own gods, completely oblivious to the customs and traditions practised by their rulers inside the cities.

The religious ideas of the Zhou aristocracy derived from the Shang practice of worshipping the king's ancestors, who were believed to be gods descending from Heaven itself. These beliefs evolved into the 'Mandate of Heaven', whereby the living king was said to have been blessed with divine status so long as his rule remained just. Meanwhile, other noble families began to worship their own ancestors and became the first people in the world to introduce surnames, enabling them to pass through successive generations, while preventing members of the same family from marrying one another. The family unit was hugely important to the Zhou and those who lost their wives and children usually had little choice but to retreat to the mountains and become bandits, stealing from travellers or raiding nearby villages. Some may even have been recruited by militant nomadic groups from the outskirts of the Zhou Empire, whose presence was becoming increasingly threatening to the regime.

In the early Eighth Century BC, King Yu fell in love with one of his concubines, Baosi, and decided to depose his wife, Queen Shen, and their son, Prince Yijiu. The queen's father, the Marquess of Shen, was outraged and conspired with the barbarous Quanrong nomads to invade the kingdom. The Zhou capital, Haojing, was captured by the invaders and Yu died in the attack, enabling Yijiu to seize the throne. The new king moved his capital to the east, but the devastation of the traditional power base by the nomads in the west had severely weakened his authority, to the extent that he required constant protection from the lords. The Zhou dynasty continued in name until the Fifth Century BC, but in reality its kings had little influence over the fiefdoms and it was only a matter of time before the lords became engulfed by civil war. One of the largest fiefdoms was the old western homeland of the Zhou, which had been recovered from the Quanrong by one of the lords. Over the following centuries, this western region, later known as Ch'in, became the most powerful state in the land, eventually lending its name to the entire country.

XXX

Thousands of years before the first European explorers arrived in their ships from across the Atlantic, the inhabitants of the Americas had already established their own civilizations without any external influence whatsoever. Having crossed the Bering Strait to enter North America from Asia about twenty thousand years ago, the earliest migrants hunted game across the continent and eventually reached Central and South America around five thousand years later, initially residing in caves. During the Third Millennium BC, tribes in Mexico cultivated crops including maize, beans and potatoes, leading to the emergence of permanent self-sufficient settlements. Gradually, the invention of agriculture spread into South America as well. In both locations the domestication of plants and animals provided the impetus for cultural developments which facilitated the earliest American civilizations.

In Mesoamerica, the first civilized societies were founded by the Olmecs; a mysterious tribe from the swampy jungles of south-eastern Mexico whose culture dominated the region for a thousand years after c.1400 BC, from religious practices to artwork and monumental architecture. It is not known what the Olmecs called themselves but their name derives from the Aztec word *Olmeca*, meaning 'people of the rubber country', where rubber was commonly produced for the famous ball-games which were played during the later Aztec period. In fact, the games were probably invented by the Olmecs themselves during the Second Millennium BC. Yet they had many more strings to their bow. Great pyramids were constructed in the centre of the vibrant Olmec cities, surrounded by colossal stone heads of their leaders and embellished with exquisite jade figurines of godlike humans and jaguars. Much of their culture and practices were to be replicated by the better known Mayan civilization which flourished centuries later.

During the formative years of Olmec civilization, the most prominent city was San Lorenzo, a cultural hub situated on the Coatzacoalcos River and controlling the surrounding agricultural land. The broad river network was conducive for trade with neighbouring regions, often by canoe, and exotic materials were shipped into the city from miles around. The great temple was located on a huge artificial plateau, overlooking a central plaza and surrounded by smaller temples and palaces, while the simpler abodes of the masses lined the lower slopes and plains. Beneath the city was an intricate stone drainage system, while colossal stone heads of their kings were on public display, each wearing helmets and graced with individualised features.

The Olmec kings appear to have legitimised their rule by claiming descent from obscure nature-gods or mythical ancestors and took part in religious rituals with the assistance of shamans. Bloodletting was common and there are indications of human sacrifice as well. Religious and cultural practices spread to other towns and cities, along with pottery styles, and the leaders at San Lorenzo may have exercised some form of political hegemony over a wide region. There is still much debate about the extent to which the Olmecs used force to establish their elevated status in Mesoamerica, but if there was such a thing as an Olmec Empire, it was not destined to be permanently ruled from San Lorenzo. Perhaps a result of an internal rebellion, sometime before 900 BC the colossal heads were pulled down and the city was left to decay, with the centre of Olmec culture shifting to the nearby city of La Venta.

The centrepiece of La Venta was a huge volcano-shaped earthwork pyramid and the wealth of the city seems to have exceeded that of San Lorenzo, with an abundance of gift offerings left behind, many of which were made from polished jade, serpentine and obsidian, imported from neighbouring regions. The ruling classes tended to associate themselves on a spiritual level with jaguars and other wild beasts, so a large proportion of the objects fashioned by the Olmec craftsmen were modelled on these sacred animals. The Olmecs of La Venta also appear to have been the first people of the Americas to create a system of writing, although the few surviving inscriptions have not been deciphered and thus far reveal nothing about the people and events which shaped Olmec civilization. Unfortunately there are many unanswered questions about these fascinating people, but their later reputation as the 'mother culture' of Mesoamerica speaks volumes for their importance. By the end of the Fifth Century BC, La Venta had been deserted as well, perhaps the result of a volcanic eruption or another natural disaster, but its legacy lived on in the civilizations that followed, most distinctively through the Maya and the Aztecs.

XXXI

The civilization of the Olmecs was long thought to be the earliest in the Western Hemisphere, but very recent discoveries in South America have changed that assumption. In the Third Millennium BC, at the same time as the Old Kingdom in Egypt, an assortment of advanced urban settlements flourished on the north-western coastline and adjacent river valleys of Peru. Over thirty sites have been identified by archaeologists, including the complex cities of Caral and Aspero, and the ancient region has since become known as the Norte Chico civilization. Extraordinarily these communities did not grow their own cereals and appear to have survived principally on fish from the sea, caught in fishing nets made from cotton that was grown in the irrigated river valleys. The staple diet consisted of clams, anchovies, mussels and sardines, supplemented by locally grown crops such as beans, peppers, squash and avocado. Trade with other communities further along the coast, or in the Amazonian jungles to the east, appears to have further stimulated the economy.

Similarly to the Olmec centres, the Norte Chico cities boasted monumental architecture in the form of stone pyramids, flat earthwork mounds and circular plazas, presumably enabling the local inhabitants to observe important ceremonial and religious rites. There were also highly concentrated residential areas, more tightly condensed than most urban areas in the ancient world. Surprisingly, despite their skill in constructing large-scale architecture, there was a notable absence of painting or sculpture. However the people of Norte Chico were proficient in textiles, made from cotton, producing clothing, bags and what appears to have been an early form of *quipu*: string-based devices that were commonly used to record quantities of food and materials during the later Inca period. They also played musical instruments, as evidenced by over thirty carved flutes that have been found in the region.

Next to nothing is known about the inner workings of Norte Chico civilization. It is generally assumed that a relatively sophisticated government and organisational structure would have been necessary to control food and cotton supplies as well as the labour required to build the central monuments, with leadership probably justified on religious grounds. However, as with the Olmecs, no evidence has been uncovered about the main characters or the precise form of government that was in place. Interestingly nothing has been found to suggest there were fortifications or warfare, indicating that the people of Norte Chico led a relatively peaceful existence. When the civilization began to decline, early in the Second Millennium BC, it does not appear to have been the result of aggression from rival tribes. Instead, it seems that people gradually began to disperse and apply irrigation techniques to less arid fertile land elsewhere. As the focus shifted away from the coastal region, the vitality of the densely populated cities disappeared. Centuries would pass before the appearance of another South American civilization to rival Norte Chico.

Indeed, the next advanced society to appear was in the northern Peruvian Andes in c.900 BC. Taking its name from the principal site, Chavín de Huántar, Chavín civilization existed over three thousand miles above sea level in the valley of the river Mosna, conveniently located for trade with other tribes in the Andean valleys to the north and south, the arid coastline to the west and the rainforest to the east. The Chavín grew crops including potatoes, quinoa and maize, while they also domesticated the llamas and alpacas which roamed in the high grasslands. Initially with a population of just a few hundred, the settlement of Chavín de Huántar grew to become an important religious and cultural centre. The focal point was the holy temple which was built of imported white granite and black limestone and situated upon elevated land, separated from the living quarters by an unoccupied zone. It contained a series of underground passages surrounding a central chamber which was decorated with images of deities, mainly in the form of jaguars and other exotic jungle animals. At the centre was a tall statue of a fanged hybrid deity known as the Lanzón, assumed to have been the supreme god. The temple served as the spiritual hub of Chavín civilization, attracting pilgrimages from miles around.

Aside from organising the construction of the temple, the leaders of the Chavín also mobilised a labour force to assemble a drainage system and network of canals. Ingeniously, they routed the canals under the temple so that during the wet season, the rush of water sounded like the roar of a jaguar. As in other Central and South American cultures, the Chavín regarded the jaguar as a sacred animal. Images of the gods, which also included supernatural beings in the form of eagles, snakes and crocodiles, were carved into stone sculptures and crafted from materials such as clay, ceramics and textiles. Similarly to other ancient civilizations, Minoan Crete for example, it seems that the experience of ritual ceremonies was enhanced by hallucinogenic drugs; in this instance from the San Pedro cactus.

Chavín culture influenced many nearby tribes, whose temples bore the hallmarks of the main temple of Chavín de Huántar, and who may have adopted some of the Chavín deities and religious practices as well as their pottery and textile techniques. Such was its importance as a pilgrimage centre that the city may have been the location of an oracle, attracting believers in their thousands. Immense power rested with the shamans who led the ritual ceremonies and controlled access to the temple and they may have ruled the city on both religious and political grounds. Although Chavín civilization declined towards the end of the First Millennium BC, its principal city remained a sacred site for later societies who owed much of their development to the ideas and practices of the Chavín.

Yet despite the legacy of the Norte Chico, Chavín and Olmec cultures in Central and South America, which provided an element of continuity to later civilizations such as the Maya, Aztec, Moche and Inca, the eventual arrival of the Europeans in the middle of the Second Millennium AD and their emphatic overpowering of native rule meant there would not be an unbroken cultural tradition from ancient to modern times as there has been in the Mediterranean, Near East, India and China. The ancient civilizations of the Americas were ultimately a series of dead ends for human development, but the stunning array of ruins and artefacts that have been left to posterity are an awe-inspiring reminder of the achievements of these people before their long isolation from the rest of the world finally came to an end.

XXXII

B y the time of the Persian invasion of Babylon in 539 BC, the world had already witnessed over three thousand years of civilization, and all this before the glory days of Greece and Rome, the zenith of the Persian Empire and the teachings of the Buddha in India or Confucius in China. Empires had risen and fallen away, famous tribes had come and gone and countless great men had lived and died. Yet whole communities in many regions of the world continued to live in the shadows, completely oblivious to the remarkable progress that had been achieved elsewhere. Over the coming centuries they too would embrace civilization, but for the time being they continued to be shackled to the prehistoric age, living in primitive agricultural settlements or continuing to lead a hunting and gathering lifestyle. This was the prevailing situation throughout the entire continents of North America and Australasia, and the vast majority of Europe and Africa.

Although they were not advanced enough to constitute civilized societies, the achievements of some primeval cultures in Europe are worth mentioning. Away from the Mediterranean sphere, the continent remained in prehistoric times until the great northerly expansion of the Roman Empire, but agriculture and metallurgy had long since arrived from Anatolia and the barbaric settlements of Europe frequently exported copper and tin via merchants from the civilized world. By the Second Millennium BC, western Europe was dominated by the ancestors of the Celts, while the northern and eastern regions consisted respectively of Germanic and Slavic tribes. These primitive, illiterate societies were led by hereditary warrior elites and completely lacked the complexities and intricacies of the developed towns and cities in the Mediterranean and Near East.

However they made their mark through a dramatic development which continues to arouse curiosity today: in western Europe there appeared a series of megalithic monuments, some of which were tombs, consisting of huge stones that had been transported from miles around and carefully arranged in circular patterns. The most famous of these sites, Stonehenge in southern Britain, was probably completed towards the end of the Second Millennium BC. Its purpose remains the source of much debate and speculation.

Yet despite these developments, the bulk of Europe to the north of the Mediterranean sphere was for the most part an irrelevance to the developed states that traded there. In fact the regions which showed the clearest signs of evolving into civilized societies were those adjacent to the existing civilizations of the ancient world. This was particularly true in southern Europe, where the customs and traditions of pre-classical Greece spread to settlements along the Mediterranean coastline. One such community was that of the Villanovans, an Iron Age people from north-western Italy who frequently traded with Greek colonists in the south and visiting Phoenician sailors. The Villanovans were the forerunners of the Etruscans, an innovative tribe whose culture and practices greatly influenced the neighbouring Latin peoples and particularly the Romans. Eventually the rest of western and central Europe would be forced to acknowledge the supremacy of the rich Mediterranean culture that began with the city-states of Greece and reached its peak of influence under the grandeur of imperial Rome.

The majesty of the classical age in the Mediterranean and its contemporary cultures in Asia produced so many beautiful artefacts and innovative ideas that it is easy to neglect the pioneering civilizations that preceded them. Yet without the ingenuity of the Mesopotamians, Egyptians, Cretans, or the people living in the valleys of the Indus and Yellow Rivers, the world would simply not be the place that it is today. The people who shaped the civilizations that existed between the Fourth Millennium and the Sixth Century

BC are not fictional characters belonging to myth and legend, but real heroes and kings whose blood continues to flow through the veins of their descendants and whose accomplishments still astonish and inspire the minds of people all over the world. As civilization continues to develop and evolve at an astounding rate, one can only hope that we never forget how it all began.